Accessorise your Mind
with Passions Inspiration and
Imagination

Angela Clare

All rights reserved. No part of this publication may be reproduced, stored in a retrieval system, or transmitted in any form or by any means, electronic, mechanical, photocopying, recording or otherwise, without the prior written permission of the author, except for brief quotations.

Cover art and design: Angela Clare

Copyright © Angela Clare 2017

Published by Accessorise your Mind 2017

ISBN: 978-1-925702-04-0

CONTENTS

CHAPTER 1 OPENING OUR MINDS — 1

Mind Accessories — 3
Why Single Them Out? — 4
Opening our Minds — 5
The Cottage of Wonders — 6
A Metaphor for our Minds — 12
Your Growing Mind — 18

CHAPTER 2 PASSIONS ACCESSORY — 21

What Will I Learn? — 24

SEARCHING FOR PASSIONS — 25

Managing Stress — 25
Using Affirmations — 27
Understanding the Issues — 28
True or False — 30
All-Encompassing Search — 31
An Interest or a Passion — 32
Childhood and Adult Passions — 36
The Influence of our Culture — 40
Passionate about a Quality — 42

PROFILE OF INTERESTS AND PASSIONS — 44

Learning from your Profile — 47

Contents

Key Points	*48*
CHAPTER 3 INSPIRATION ACCESSORY	**51**
What Will I Learn?	*53*
SOURCES OF INSPIRATION	**53**
BITE SIZE TASTERS	**56**
THE RESONANCE OF INSPIRATION	**69**
Inspiration at the Theatre	*71*
Tangible and Intangible	*73*
CREATING	**75**
Arriving without Looking	*81*
Acting on Inspiration	*81*
People who Inspire	*83*
An Inspirational Sourcebook	*85*
A Selection of Sources	*86*
APPLYING	**89**
INTERPRETING	**97**
Different Interpretations of a Painting	*99*
RADIAL AND LINEAR	**104**
Radial Approach	*105*
Linear Record	*109*
CONCLUSION	**114**
Key Points	*115*

CHAPTER 4 IMAGINATION ACCESSORY — 119
What Will I Learn? — 121

ASPECTS OF MEMORY — 123
Visual Memory — 123
Memory of Senses and Emotions — 126
Memory of Non-Reality Images & Senses — 128
Curiosity — 129

VISUAL MEMORY — 130
Authentic and Adapted Visualisation — 134
Seeing in our Minds — 138
Speed and Clarity — 142

SENSUAL & EMOTIONAL MEMORY — 143
Imagining TTSS Senses — 144
Imagining Emotions — 146

THE DIVERSITY OF IMAGINATION — 150
Conscious and Subconscious — 150
Dreaming — 152
Three Ways of Connecting with Sleeping Dreams — 154
Sleepy Dream States — 157
Novels — 159
Exploring Novel Imagination — 160
Music — 163

Creating	*167*
Memorising	*169*
Motivating	*172*
Rehearsing	*175*
Sport	*179*
Relaxing	*181*
SELECTIONS AND VIEWS	**183**
Selecting a Surface	*183*
Viewing angles in our minds	*188*
ADAPTING THE WAY WE THINK	**190**
Applying Imaginative Thinking	*193*
Options	*197*
OPENING OUR MINDS	**198**
Exercise 1 – Observe, Record, Adapt	*199*
Exercise 2 – Sharpen your Visualisation Skills	*201*
Exercise 3 – Look for the Details	*201*
Exercise 4 – Use Trigger Words	*202*
Exercise 5 – Add Senses and Emotions	*202*
CONCLUSION	**204**
Key Points	*205*
Meet the Author	**213**
Endnotes	*217*

CHAPTER 1 OPENING OUR MINDS

We've all had those moments in our lives when we try to think of the answer to a question. We rack our minds again and again but our brain just won't seem to function. We try to *force* our minds to come up with the answer, but we don't know how to *access* that answer. A good example of trying to rack our minds for answers is the way Charlotte Bronte describes the feelings of Jane Eyre as she searches her mind for new directions:

> "I sat up in bed by way of arousing this said brain: it was a chilly night; I covered my shoulders with a shawl, and then I proceeded to think again with all my might.
> What do I want? A new place, in a new house, amongst new faces, under new circumstances: I want this because it is of no use wanting anything better. How do people do to get a new place? They apply to friends, I suppose: I have no friends. There are many others who have no friends, who must look about for themselves and be their own helpers;

and what is their resource?

I could not tell: nothing answered me; I then ordered my brain to find a response, and quickly. It worked and worked faster: I felt the pulses throb in my head and temples; but for nearly an hour it worked in chaos, and no result came of its efforts. Feverish with vain labour, I got up and took a turn in the room; un-drew the curtain, noted a star or two, shivered with cold, and again crept to bed."[1]

Jane Eyre was trying to force her mind to think of her next purpose in life, to answer the question "where to from here?" She felt that if she could concentrate long enough on the question that she would eventually come up with the answer, and while she *did* come up with an answer, it took her a long time to get there. Part of the reason why it takes us so long to come up with answers is because we don't understand our minds sufficiently and we don't always access our minds in the right way. We rack our minds when we can't find the answers to a question, or when the answers don't come quickly enough. So we might wonder what our passions are and just think and think in the hope that something might pop into our minds, or we might try to work out what inspires us the most and hope that our minds will respond with something.

When we search for answers, we can sometimes do this without a sufficient understanding of what we're searching for or what we hope to gain from our answers. So instead of just racking our minds to find answers, we can of course start with an approach of first to **understand** the issue, second to **access** our thoughts, and third to **apply** our thoughts. If we use this **three step approach** in searching for answers, we can at least give ourselves the opportunity to come up with more answers than if we just forced our minds to think or to 'hope' that the answers will magically appear. Accessorise your Mind uses this principle of understanding first, accessing second, and applying third, and then applies this to important qualities in our lives, such as Passions, Inspiration and Imagination, qualities that enable us to pursue our dreams, progress with our lives, and discover our individuality as well as our commonality.

Mind Accessories

Each of the qualities which are described as Mind Accessories, such as Relaxation and Energy, are termed 'Accessories' because we can choose when we want to have them in our minds. We can choose how we want to use them. So just as a fashion accessory is to clothing, so a 'Mind Accessory' is to our brain. When we use our Mind Accessories, then using the three step approach of understanding first, accessing second, and applying third will help us to learn how to use them more effectively. And as you learn about each Accessory, you will take your mind on a journey and begin to understand and explore a variety of thoughts and ideas. It's then up to you to put each of your Accessories into practice.

Through your Accessories you will have the opportunity to stimulate different areas of your mind and learn more about yourself and the world around you. And when you *engage* with your own personal journey, the impact of what you learn will be far greater than just reading a list of 'so called' answers. When you learn to Accessorise your Mind, you will have the ability to open mental doors…..when you open mental doors, you will have the opportunity to open physical doors…..and when you open physical doors, you will discover many new worlds previously unknown to you.

Why Single Them Out?

I want to briefly explain why Mind Accessories are singled out as separate qualities. Consider a watercolour painting of a single yellow flower on a white background. At first glance, it's just another picture of a yellow flower, but as you take the time to look at the painting in more detail, you notice there are variations in the colour of the flower, some areas catch the light and are bright in colour, while other areas are in shadow and have a duller though still luminous quality. Then you notice the texture of the flower. The petals seem to have a smooth appearance, you can almost feel them, and the shape of the petals are not exactly the same as you'd thought at first glance, each have their own unique shape, some petals are longer than others, some are curling over and others are curling under. By now you've noticed differences in colour, tone, transparency, texture, shape, and other special attributes, and because there is nothing else around the flower to distract your mind, you can concentrate on the qualities of the flower. This principle of limiting distractions from our minds is the same one that's used for each Accessory. Because each Accessory is isolated from other distractions, we can focus on one Accessory at a time and attempt to *understand* its qualities in greater detail. We can then *access* our thoughts and *apply* our Accessories in a more informed and valuable way.

Opening our Minds

Throughout the Mind Accessory books I make a number of references to 'opening our minds', and by this I mean becoming more aware of what is around us and expanding the different areas of our minds so that we can learn and grow. Much of the time we can become accustomed to 'living on the surface'. We don't really explore who we are, and we don't really 'see' the world around us. We become very accustomed to the way things are through the routine and various stresses of our lives, much of which can consume a significant amount of our time and thoughts. While our routine might also involve various interests and pastimes, we can still become very mentally 'stuck' with our minds and become closed to those things that are outside the world we have defined for ourselves. Using our Mind Accessories is a way of opening our minds so that we can explore our thoughts, see the life around us in a different way, and allow ourselves to grow mentally. Growing mentally enables us to be more independent, more assured, and more aware of the opportunities around us.

If we actively search beyond our everyday living experience, then we can find new meanings in our lives, we can explore our minds and the way we are, and we can explore and question the things we accept. By continually growing in this way we can keep reaching towards what we seek, and by learning about other people's experiences, we can examine our own lives and put them into perspective. Learning to open our minds is a way of empowering ourselves as we move forwards throughout our lives. If we don't explore, expand, and use the abilities of our minds, then we won't even know what's there. We won't know what we're missing.

The Cottage of Wonders

To continue with the theme of opening our minds and becoming more aware of what's around us, I'm now going to take you on a quick journey to 'The Cottage of Wonders'. It's a story about a cottage which has been closed up for some time, but which gains a new lease of life when the owner decides to reawaken it. The story is used as a metaphor for our minds, where the cottage represents our minds, and the reawakening of the cottage represents the way we can explore and use our minds and open up new possibilities:

> I was on my way to visit a cottage I hadn't seen for some time. The last time I was there was as a child. I remember many happy times running around with my uncle's dog, and playing board games in the lounge with my two cousins. My uncle sold the cottage when I was a teenager, but having retained such fond memories of the place, I resolved I would try to buy it if it came up on the market. One day, my dream finally came true, and I became the new owner of this wonderful cottage, the only problem was that my work would keep me away from the place for a full year. I had placed some of my furniture and belongings in the cottage, and draped white dustsheets over as much as I could. If only I'd known it would have been a full year before I would return then I might have made other plans.
>
> On this day when I would again reunite with my cottage, I had caught a bus from Broomhill and was now walking the short distance that led to my home. It was a rather

grey day as I walked along the neighbouring streets. It had been raining that morning and the sun was struggling to push its way between the clouds. As I approached the cottage, I noticed more intently the recognisable white washed walls, small casement windows with turquoise painted frames, and the traditional dark thatched roof. It had a small front porch that consisted of a grey slate roof and white lattice side details on knee high wall supports. The walls and the lattice were also painted white.

Looking at the cottage from several metres away, I thought I could see a light on, but I couldn't understand how that could be possible. Eventually, I arrived at the small wooden gate that provided the entrance to my country garden. At first, I had some difficulty in opening the gate as the rain had long since rusted its hinges, but it finally relented, and I walked along the wet and dark grey slate path right up to the turquoise front door. I grasped a set of keys from my coat pocket and searched for the front door key. It was easy to recognise as it was a large old fashioned key, one that seemed more appropriate for a mansion than for my small cottage. Having found the said key, I turned it in the lock and the door opened with a few creaks, groans, and noticeable cobwebs.

The layout inside was quite simple. A small hallway allowed access to the front lounge on the left, the dining area to the right, and the kitchen-come-laundry straight ahead. All three bedrooms and single bathroom were located upstairs.

I entered the front lounge, but it was difficult to make any sense of identity or warmth in the room since the dustsheets covered almost everything. The room was rather dark, but I noticed a bright shaft of light penetrating its way through one of the windows. Suddenly, I realised why I had seen a light from the cottage. A small shaft of sunlight had struggled to enter the house between a gap in the lounge curtains and had met with a small circular wall mirror. This in turn was reflecting the light back onto the street. It seemed to be the only area of brightness in the whole room.

I set about reawakening my cottage and started opening all the curtains to let the now prevalent sunshine stream into the interior. I also opened a few windows to freshen up the air. Already I felt better, and I could see the potential of the place. I could also see how dusty and cobwebbed the interior had become, and there seemed to be such a lack of colour everywhere. Everything seemed to take on a shade of sepia.

I continued in earnest to reawaken my

home. Having located some cleaning brushes and cloths in the cupboard under the stairs, I began to sweep away the cobwebs, sweep the timber floors, and shake all the rugs outside. Next came the dustsheets which I rolled up very carefully so as not to create any more dust. These too got shaken outside. As I walked back into my cottage I could at last see some colour. In the lounge I could see a rosy red three-seater settee, the blues and yellows of a large central rug, and a collection of carved wooden animals on the white framed mantelpiece. I had discovered the carvings in a box next to the mantelpiece and had decided to display them straight away as they were so unusual and interesting. More colour became apparent in the kitchen as I rediscovered a light timber dresser, and in this I placed some blue and white dinner plates. The kitchen displayed cream wall tiles with occasional depictions of fruits, such as pears, apples, blackberries, and plums. In the dining room I could see the texture and detail of the dining table and chairs. I had bought them about a year ago at an antiques fair. Everything was beginning to come alive and take its place in my new home.

Having scrubbed, dusted, swept, and polished for several hours I felt a tinge of hunger arrive, so I took myself to the kitchen and unpacked some groceries that a neighbour had kindly purchased for me. I constructed a ham sandwich as best I could, being limited only to a fork and spoon. All the other cutlery was packed away somewhere in one of the many boxes in the house. I then made myself a coffee and returned to the lounge where I could sit and eat in comfort. When my stomach was satisfied, I sat quietly for a while examining the new found colour and remembered ornaments that I had just uncovered. I looked over at one of the windows and watched a couple of SAS spiders descend from the top casement window, right to the bottom, and beyond my gaze. I felt the warmth of the sun as it filled the room and intensified the colours, both inside and out.

I walked over to one of the open windows and watched the birds as they suspiciously darted about. Twitching their little heads, they would listen and look for anything that might alarm, and fly away if there was even the slightest sense of danger. I could smell some of the flowers as the warmth of the sun reignited their aroma, and I could even feel the touch of the sun on my face. I looked at the path I had walked up so many times as a child and seemed to notice for the very first time how the grey paving was actually a mixture of fine streaks of colour, with pinks, greens, and blues all intermixed. The more I looked, the more features I could see.

A Metaphor for our Minds

As I mentioned above, the story of The Cottage of Wonders is used as a metaphor for our minds. Just as the cottage lays dormant and undisturbed for some time, we can also leave areas of our minds dormant and undisturbed. This can often be the case if we become caught up in the routine of our lives, or if our minds become overly consumed by stress or worry. We use our minds every day, but we don't always 'see', 'sense' or 'feel' beyond what we are used to or what we consider 'normal' for our lives. This is where our Cottage of Wonders (or areas of our minds) can become subdued, unused and undiscovered. The good news is that we always have the opportunity to reawaken different areas of our minds even if we haven't used them for some time. The way we can do this is to use our 'Mind Accessories', so that we can learn to see our world in a different way and become much more aware of the variety of life around us. Our Cottage of Wonders, then, is like the wonders we can explore and discover in our minds.

The finer metaphorical details of our Cottage of Wonders are somewhat hidden. It's easy to get caught up in the details of the story alone, but if we look beyond the story and search for the various ways it might apply to our minds, then we can begin to see some of the links. The following is an explanation of those finer metaphorical details and the way they can apply to different areas of our minds:

The first mention of the cottage is about the memories of childhood. Life seemed less complicated then and happiness sprang from simple pleasures, such as running with a dog, or playing board games. As children, our pleasures or passions run wild and free and we aren't hung up by the pressures of adulthood. It's a time when we tend to use our imagination much more and role play with scenes such as pirates and storybook heroes. As we become adults, we often lose our strong sense of passion and wild imagination, and many of our simple pleasures can become forgotten. This is partly because we have responsibilities as an adult, and also because we want to move on from childhood and into a new era of growth. The message here, though, is that if we are searching for qualities such as passions and imagination, then one of the first ports of call is to return to our childhood memories, and to uncover some of the aspirations we had as a child.

Another metaphorical detail of the story is where the narrator describes how work had kept them away from their cottage for a full year. This is symbolic of the way we can consider our work and routine to be more important than uncovering and discovering areas of our minds, and ultimately different areas of our lives. We can become so engrossed in our work and routine that we can forget to think about what we really want to do with our lives. So on the day the narrator is to be reunited with their cottage, this is like the day when we decide to explore our minds and to open up new thoughts and ideas.

Continuing through the story, we are told that it's rather a cloudy day when the owner is to again reunite with their cottage, but as they progress towards their home, the sun begins to struggle through the clouds. This is symbolic of the way we can begin to 'see the light' as different aspects of our world suddenly become clearer in our minds, and we can move forwards with hope.

The story then moves on to the details of the house. The owner arrives at a small wooden gate and as expected they need a little force to push it open. This relates to the way we can try to *access* our thoughts when the answers don't come easily. We need to open various 'gateways' to our minds, but if the gateways to our thoughts have been closed for some time, then a certain amount of mental effort and determination is needed to re-open them again. It's like going back to study as a mature age student, since it takes a lot of mental energy and determination to get back into the swing of things.

When the narrator finally arrives at their front door, they search for a large key. The symbolisms here are the key and the act of unlocking the door. The key represents a particular method for opening our minds, while unlocking the door represents our decision to consciously unlock our minds. The size of the key is also significant. We might think that our minds, or our intelligence, is limited and therefore requires just a small key, but in fact we have the opportunity to open our minds to the capacity of a mansion. We shouldn't limit the ability to open our minds by what we *think* our capacity for learning might be (a capacity which someone might have told us but which isn't necessarily true for ourselves). Another important symbolism is the description of the key as being old fashioned. This is because when we learn for our future, we also need to learn about our past.

Having entered the cottage, the internal layout is described and then the narrator begins to reawaken their home. This is symbolic of the way we can begin to define new areas of our minds and uncover our true potential. We can also attempt to move away from the 'sepia colour' of our lives and into a life of infinite colour.

Another important feature of the story is when the narrator notices a light coming from the cottage. They first see the light before entering their home. Reference to the light is symbolic in a number of ways. One of these can be allied to the well known expression 'the lights are on but no one's home' since we can be so busy with our everyday lives that we can't see anything beyond them. Another symbolism relates more directly to the shaft of sunlight that passes through one of the lounge windows, then onto a small circular mirror, and then reflected back onto the street. This latter description relates to the way we can reflect back what we learn or what we 'think' we know, but we also have to be aware of opening our minds to our *own* ideas and thoughts. The inclusion in the story of the small circular mirror is also a reference to the mirror shown in the wonderful painting "The Arnolfini Marriage", a painting through which we can discover more the further we look.[2]

Now we are familiar with some of the details of the cottage, the story goes on to describe the physical exertion of cleaning and reawakening the place. The physical exertion of cleaning is like the mental energy we have to expend if we are to broaden our minds and really *use* our minds. It takes hard work and commitment if we are to really gain more from our lives, and to see the world through different eyes.

As the cleaning and dusting continues in the cottage, the identity of each room becomes much clearer. The furniture and personal ornaments that are uncovered contribute towards this identity. This emergence of identity relates to the way we can get to know ourselves better by understanding and applying our Mind Accessories. When we think with our Mind Accessories, we can spend time with them and begin to uncover the individuality which makes each of us unique.

Finally, we come to the symbolism of hunger. When the narrator talks about feeling hungry and makes a ham sandwich, this represents the way we might hunger and thirst to 'know the unknown'. We need to have an appetite and a desire to learn if we want to uncover the unknown. The story notes that the narrator had a spoon instead of a knife for constructing the ham sandwich. This translates symbolically to tell us that even if we don't start with the right tools in life, we can still try to achieve what we desire. So, for example, if someone has a limited school education in literature or science, this shouldn't stop them from pursuing these subjects at a later date if they desire. We shouldn't believe that we don't have the correct mental skills to do something. Instead, we can choose to use our minds better, unlock those areas of our minds that can lead us forwards, and combine this with personal motivation to achieve what we want to achieve.

Towards the end of the story, the narrator is

rewarded by feeling the warmth of the sun and by enjoying the aroma of the flowers. We too can find rewards through our Mind Accessories by discovering more about ourselves and our lives, and by opening up new dreams and possibilities.

Your Growing Mind

I want to mention a brief note here on what can happen when you gain experience in using your Mind Accessories. As you continue to understand and use them, you may notice that your mind is beginning to function in a different way. For example, when you Accessorise your Mind with Imagination, you may discover that your mind is naturally becoming more imaginative and that you are beginning to see things in a different way. You might start to write a short story, a poem, or the lyrics to a song. When you look at the scenery from the bus you catch every day, your journey may become more interesting as you focus on something that stimulates your imagination. You might begin to visualise a story line for what you see around you and discover a level of detail that you were completely unaware of. When you Accessorise your Mind with Passions, you may become enthused in an interest you had never thought of pursuing in your wildest dreams. This can partly be attributed to your growing mind and your expanded thoughts and possibilities.

The Journey

Time has brought me to this place,
Unrelenting in its pace;
My mind conceives,
My thoughts collide,
Take a breath for here we ride.

Let's speak through mirrors and see through sands,
Move through mountains and desert lands,
Find the magic of our lives,
Feel the freedom in our eyes.

Let's keep on going through rough and smooth,
Dedication and time will prove.

CHAPTER 2   PASSIONS ACCESSORY

A strong enthusiasm and desire for something

Our passions can take many different forms. Some people are passionate about a cause, some are passionate about their career, many are passionate about their family, and some are passionate about creating. Others are passionate about music and might collect memorabilia to keep their passions alive. Many are passionate about collecting certain objects, such as watches, model cars, antiques, or crystals. Our list of passions can go on and on because the possibilities are so endless, and we can have numerous passions throughout our lives.

Passions can be divided into many different branches and specialties. Take a passion for food as an example. Some people are passionate about cooking food, while others are passionate about eating it. Some people are passionate about the presentation of food, so that meals are as pleasing to the eye as they are to the palette. Some people grow their own fruit and vegetables and are passionate about that extra special taste that only home grown food can provide.

Many others are passionate about buying organic food or free range produce.

The passions for sport are also a diverse example. Swimming, running, football, rugby, baseball, squash, hockey, cricket, darts, snooker…thousands of different sport are pursued around the world. And an example of the way passions can connect with sport is the experience of a large scale sporting event, such as the Olympic Games. Millions of people 'tune in' to the Olympic Games and many of those who aren't usually enthusiastic about sport can become involved in the whole experience. These large scale events can instil a sense of national pride and can additionally raise our passions as we support the athletes who represent our country:

> As I sit in the Olympic stadium I am aware of the sounds around me, of chanting, clapping, and drums, and the rise of unrestrained energy as people overflow with excitement and anticipation. I can almost *taste* the passion in the air as I feel the intensity of the athletes and the enthusiasm of the crowd. I look around me and see groups of people waving flags. Slogans are written on cloth sheets or large pieces of card and are waved around the crowd. As the passions grow ever stronger, I join in with a Mexican wave that runs right around the stadium. As I stand up, my heart races and I feel alive. I become bonded with this amazing, unifying experience.

It's clear that we can be extremely passionate about sport, and our emotions and senses can become heightened to a higher level than our normal everyday living experience. When we watch our favourite sporting events on television we can become very passionate. We might even find ourselves shouting out loud for the athletes or teams we support as we attempt to urge them on. We can also find ourselves tensing up at critical stages, or feeling elated when our athletes or team enjoy a win.

With this brief overview of passions, we can now come to the critical question. If we know there are numerous passions to be found in the world, with numerous specialities and diversities, why is it that so many of us can feel a lack of passion in our lives and wonder if we can ever find just *one* passion? This is the big question. The answers lie partly with the way we view our passions, that is, we might not recognise a passion when we have it in our lives. Another clue is the way we can become embroiled in the stress and routine of our lives to the point where we lose the sensation of passions; we lose the *feeling* of being passionate. We can also discover, to our amazement, that part of the reason for our lack of passions is that we haven't made time for them. This might sound a ridiculous thing to say, but in order to find and keep our passions alive we have to make time for them.

Passions are extremely important in our living experience. They help us to 'refuel' on a mental, physical and emotional level, and can invigorate our mental outlook and sense of well-being. When we share our passions with other liked-minded people, we can enjoy them at an even greater level. So let's explore this amazing Accessory and see what we can discover.

What Will I Learn?

If we know there are a variety of passions out there in the world, then how do we discover the passions that are personal to us, those that might give us a sense of fulfilment and energy, maybe even a sense of purpose? This is where your Passions Accessory comes into play. By taking yourself through the following pages, and by undertaking the various exercises, you will begin to gain a clearer understanding of what passions can really mean in your life, and how you can endeavour to search for them. You will learn about some of the ways your mind can block your view when searching for passions, and you will be given some techniques for overcoming these difficulties. You will learn about the differences between an 'interest' and a 'passion', and you will begin to uncover your awareness of passions through your senses and emotions. And you will learn about some of the 'spin offs' that passions can provide, such as strengthening your personal qualities of determination and stamina.

When you get to the section entitled 'Profile of Interests and Passions', this will give you the opportunity to research your interests and passions and to open up your mind to new possibilities. Various prompters are used to assist you with this, including a number of themes designed to jog your thoughts.

SEARCHING FOR PASSIONS

Managing Stress

Being passionate about something is one of our strongest emotions and it's also one of our strongest sources of inner energy, but it can also be one of our most elusive. Among the considerations for this elusiveness is whether the amount of **stress** in our lives is affecting our ability to see our passions. We don't want to eliminate stress completely because a certain amount of stress can be positive. For example, feeling stressed about giving a speech to a crowd can cause our adrenalin levels to rise and our energy levels to increase, and this in turn can assist us in giving a strong presentation, and it also has the potential to be a passionate presentation. On the other hand, constantly high levels of stress, or badly managed stress, can make us feel tired, lack lustre and emotionally drained. It can affect our ability to think because we aren't allowing our minds to relax, 'let go' or recharge. This in turn can impact on our search for passions because our minds can be subdued by stress, and we can feel that we only have the ability to cope with our everyday lives, and nothing more. So the first step in the search for our passions is to assess the amount of stress in our lives, and to decide whether we need to re-prioritise what is important. 'Clearing the decks' in this way can help us to move forwards and gain much more from our lives.

Is stress subduing your mind and your search for passions?
Have a think about what you find stressful in your life. Ask yourself the following:

1) Am I worrying myself about issues that just need to take their own time to resolve?
2) Have I organised how to deal with each of my stressful sources by breaking them down into manageable 'bite size pieces' and by using a step by step approach?
3) Can I reduce the amount of stress in my life by changing my lifestyle?

The above questions are just a few initial prompters to help you think about the various forms of stress in your life. There are numerous books published on the subject of stress, so I won't go into any further detail here. Suffice it to say that we can potentially worry ourselves about anything and everything, so we have to learn to **manage what worries us** and what we feel stressed about. We also have to **organise our lives** so that we can deal with stress in a way that is less subduing to our minds, and then turn our stress into something more positive, so that our stresses become our 'challenges' and our 'goals' rather than our problems.

Using Affirmations

The next consideration in the search for our passions is to think about what we are telling ourselves in our minds. Let's imagine that someone is saying in their mind *'I don't know what my passions are and I don't know how to find them.'* They end up repeating this statement over and over again in their minds and they also tell some of their friends that they can't find their passions. While this person might think that repeating a phrase such as this is a step in the right direction (because they are actually thinking about what their passions might be), their phrase can become self-fulfilling because they can end up convincing themselves that they don't have any passions and they aren't likely to ever find them. **Repeating phrases in our minds**, or out loud, can powerfully change the way we think (this is why affirmations are such a useful tool), but just remember that repetition can be negative as well as positive. We have to be aware of *what* we are telling ourselves and *what* we are convincing ourselves. If we keep repeating negative phrases in our minds then we can actually 'block' part of our minds and affect our ability to seek what we want.

Are negative mental phrases blocking your mind and your passions?
1) Do you repeat negative phrases in your mind? Try to define them.
2) Are any of your negative phrases restricting you from seeking your passions?

The next step in the process of unblocking your mind is to resolve to turn around your negative mental phrases and make them into positive phrases. For example, a negative phrase of 'I can't find my passions' becomes 'I will find my passions and I will actively look for them'. Once you have established your positive phrases, list them together and keep them somewhere prominent. You will then have a regular reminder of all your positive actions.

Understanding the Issues

Another area we have to think about is the way we can tend to **lump everything into one basket**, so that many people say they are looking for their passions, but they are actually absorbing many other issues into this one search. Let's look at the example of Catherine to explain this more clearly. Catherine isn't very happy in her office job. She feels she has more to offer the world. She wants to find some meaning in her life, to feel useful, and to dedicate her energies towards 'something'. She also wants to feel a sense of stability and security. She decides she must try to find out what her passions are so that her life might be taken in a different direction, one that might be filled with a sense of energy and enthusiasm. Catherine convinces herself that finding her passions will be the answer to everything, nothing else will do, and until she finds them, she can't really start living her life.

Now let's look at the story from another angle. If Catherine alternatively decided to distinguish the separate areas of her life which are of concern to her, then she can think about how she might deal with them individually. Her search for passions can be one of her goals, but it will not be the sole solution to *all* of her problems. She could assess her skills and qualifications and either investigate other options at her current work place, or try to find a new job that will give her more satisfaction. She can think about the reasons why she seeks stability and security and come up with some options. It may be that she's renting a flat and wants to buy her own home, or that she wants a job with a regular income rather than one that just pays on commission. She can also think about particular causes that hold a special meaning for her, such as the protection of animals or protection of the environment. Catherine has many issues to consider and she has to identify them separately if she wants to understand the reasons for her worry. She can then decide on her options and choices and move forwards with her chosen actions.

Are you absorbing other issues into your search for passions?

1) Does your search for passions also involve various concerns in your life? Identify what those concerns may be.
2) If you have a list of concerns, begin to identify all the options that are possible for resolving them or moving them forwards in a positive direction.
3) Choose an option for each of your concerns and then make a commitment to *act* on each of your chosen options. You might not be able to physically get started on each of your chosen options straight away, as you may have to consult with others, or get information on a particular issue, but you do have the opportunity to make a 'mental' commitment to your options.

True or False

There is another human tendency that we need to think about, and that is the one where we place our desire for passions into our work, so that our work becomes a **self-fulfilling passion**. Later on down the track, we might suddenly 'wake up' and find out that our work was a false passion and that we were subduing our true passions all along. There are of course many people whose work is also their true passion, but for others their work can become a false passion. If we spend most of our time involved in our work and don't engage in other activities, then we may not even realise that our true passions lie elsewhere.

Are you in a self-fulfilling passion?
1) Do you spend much of your time thinking about and engaging in your work?
2) Are you really passionate about your work or is it a self-fulfilling passion?
3) Given the choice, would you rather spend time at work or with something you're really passionate about?

All-Encompassing Search

The final aspect to consider is the way we can become lulled into the idea of looking for '*One*' passion. It's '*The*' passion, the one thing that represents who we are, that fulfils us, that gives us meaning......and there's only room for one of these passions in our lives. Some people decide that this One passion has to be some amazing revelation that will change the whole course of their lives. They raise up their search for this **One elusive passion** until their desire reaches such a high level that they can't see all the other opportunities for passions around them. We have to move away from the idea of seeking out just 'One' all-encompassing passion, and we have to redefine the role of our passions. We have the opportunity for many passions in our lives and they don't have to be magnificent in the eyes of others. Our passions are for *us* to define and for *us* to enjoy.

Are you looking for One elusive passion?
1) What are you hoping to find in a passion? Think about why you're looking for your passions, such as fulfilment, excitement, and achievement.
2) Can *One* passion realistically fulfil all the things you're hoping to find?
3) Is your search for one passion driven by your desire to fulfil other people's opinions of you?

We need to think about having many different passions in our lives rather than just 'One' all-encompassing passion. We might end up dedicating much of our time to a single passion, but that shouldn't limit us from finding other smaller passions in our lives…they're out there somewhere.

An Interest or a Passion

By now you might be asking the question *"how can I tell the difference between an interest and a passion?"* Generally speaking, our 'interests' are those things we **like to do**, but our passions are those things we **love to do**, they are important to us, we can't get enough of them, they are in fact 'the interests' we take to a higher level. The reason for distinguishing between our interests and passions is that we can start to understand the roles they play in our lives, and in turn, we can begin to identify the **clues** that can lead us towards our passions.

One of the most striking differences between our interests and passions are the **emotions** we feel. Being passionate is a strong emotion in its own right, and this highlights the far stronger emotions we feel for our passions in comparison to those we feel for our interests. We can feel enthusiasm, pleasure, contentment and excitement with both our passions and our interests, but the **intensities** of those emotions are far stronger with our passions.

Of course, not all the emotions we feel with our passions and interests are positive ones. We can also experience negative emotions, such as frustration, sadness, impatience and annoyance. This is particularly the case when we've put a lot of effort into something and it doesn't turn out the way we had hoped. For example, it could be a short story you've written that just doesn't sound right, so you end up rewriting the whole thing, or maybe the pottery you put in the kiln was damaged, so you had to start all over again.

The ups and downs of our emotions are greatest with our passions because it's these that usually **mean more to us** – we can choose to 'let go' of some of our interests when we get fed up with them, but we are much more determined to keep hold of our passions.

We will often choose to *work* with our passions and take ourselves through the rough and the smooth. We also learn to deal with the more 'challenging' emotions that our passions can provide (such as a feeling of failure) as well as enjoy the more positive emotions. The clue here is that we can try to find some of our passions by raising our **emotional awareness** of passions. By being more aware of the type and intensity of emotions involved in passions, we can give ourselves a better opportunity for seeking them out.

> *Raise your emotional awareness of passions:*
> 1) Can you think of an interest that could become a passion because it's something you really enjoy?
> 2) Have you ever had a passion for something but gave it up because it was too frustrating?

In the same way that our emotions can become more intense with our passions, our **senses** can also become more heightened. Some of our senses are naturally heightened by the nature of our passions, such as someone who has a passion for painting becoming more conscious of what they 'really' see when they attempt a painting, or someone who enjoys carpentry becoming more aware of their sense of touch, feeling the texture of the wood and the joints between the timbers. Sometimes we enjoy a passion precisely because it involves our senses, such as someone who has a passion for the aroma of a scented garden, or someone who has a passion for the taste of certain wines. So our senses can be the **by-product of our passions**, because our senses are heightened, or they can be **part of what fuels our passions**, because they are a key reason for our enjoyment.

Raise your sensual awareness of passions:
1) Describe one sound that you feel passionate about, such as a piece of music, the sound of the sea, or the sound of an animal.
2) Describe one taste that gives you pleasure, such as croissants, custard, curries, salads, chocolate, or nuts. (You won't necessarily be overly passionate about a particular food, but the idea here is to raise your *awareness* of the tastes you enjoy).
3) Describe one image that makes you feel passionate, such as a rain forest, the countryside, an old castle, or a moonlit evening.

In summary, we can have many interests and passions in our lives. It comes down to how we define them, and whether we are prepared to stick with them through the rough and the smooth. We might let go of a passion because we think it's not supposed to be frustrating and should be enjoyable all the time. But we know that passions are always going to have their ups and downs, so we have to learn to take ourselves through the more difficult periods and give our passions the opportunity to grow.

Childhood and Adult Passions

The passions we experience as a child are different to the passions we experience and look for as an adult. When we're children, we become easily engrossed in something we love to do, so much so, that many of our childhood passions seem very simple when we look back on them through adult eyes:

A Passion for Katy

When Katy was nine years old she had a passion for horses. She bought a book about horses and learnt about the Palomino, Arab, Shire and Shetland….she could identify the Pinto, Strawberry Roan, Appaloosa and Haflinger, and she read about all the countries they came from. She put up a poster on her bedroom wall. It was a group of white horses rushing towards her, their white manes flying in the air and water dancing and sparkling at their feet. In her imagination they represented a sense of adventure, wild and free, strong and yet graceful. She longed to live her dream, to ride on a magnificent horse, to feel the wind rushing through her hair, and to jump over high fences and hedges.

First came the gear. She acquired a crop and

hard hat and would display them proudly when she ran around the garden, pretending to trot like a horse and jumping over one of several sticks she had placed like hurdles on the ground. She dreamed of entering gymkhanas, and becoming world famous for achieving the highest hurdle ever attempted, moving gracefully and skilfully with her trusty horse, Cristabel.

When she was eleven years old she finally had the opportunity to go horse riding. She was so excited, she could finally 'live the dream' and experience the adventure and excitement of her passion. What a feeling of elation as she sat on a horse for the first time, this was really happening after all, she would finally be galloping through fields and jumping over fences, just as she had dreamed.

It was a little hard at first to get used to the size of the horse and the way her legs had to stretch over the saddle, but Katy didn't care because she was finally the adventurer, the heroine, the world famous show jumper. The saddle was quite hard as they trotted through the country lanes and her bottom got quite sore. Up down, up down, as her bottom planted itself firmly on the saddle then up again in the air. This wasn't anything like she thought it would be, but she knew the best bit was to come, when she would finally canter through the fields and be wild and free.

As each person waited their turn to canter she recalled a scene from one of her favourite books – *'Riding with gusto through the green fields of the countryside she felt the fresh air bring life to her face. She could see the beauty of the fields around her, and felt such a sense of wonder and happiness.'* When it was finally her turn to canter, the horse shot off without any help from her, and she was slipping and sliding all over the place as she tried to stay on the saddle. Her mind was thinking solely about hanging on as tight as she could and trying to make it to the other side without falling off.

Finally, after an exhausting couple of hours, her first horse riding experience was complete. She dismounted rather ungainly, but what a shock, her legs felt like they bowed out in the shape of the horse, and her bottom, boy did that ache! Despite these unexpected pains, she persevered with a few more riding experiences, but jiggling up and down in the saddle just didn't seem to fulfil the dream of her passion. One day, as she came to the end of another riding experience, she dismounted from her horse, and as she walked back to the stable she began to muse to herself *"hmmm....this horse riding lark doesn't feel like I'm 'living the dream'....all this bumping up and down, sore bottom and bruises....and the horse seems to have a will of its own, we're just not 'in tune' with each other as I thought we'd be....it's not a bit like my adventure books. Hmmm.... I think I'm going to change my passion....instead of horse riding I'm going to be passionate about something beautiful and romantic, something delicate and graceful ....yes, that's it, my new passion is going to be....ballet!"*

As a child we select a whole array of different passions, and somehow it's easier for us to choose because we go with the flow, we either love them or we don't. And as a child we often allow our imagination to run wild when we think about our passions, even if we haven't had much experience with them. One of the problems when we're adults is that we tend to overcomplicate what we're looking for. We forget the simplicity and enjoyment of what we loved to do as a child. Our outlook as an adult will obviously be different to our outlook as a child, but that doesn't mean we can't return to some of our childhood passions and take them to a more mature level. We always have the choice to take the 'seed' of a childhood passion and see where it might take us as an adult.

As well as rekindling some of our childhood interests, we can also use the principle of 'simplifying what we're looking for' and apply it to our everyday experiences to discover some of our simplest of pleasures, such as a love of the ocean, or a walk in the park. If we identify our simplest of pleasures, we can begin to point ourselves in the right direction and start to understand what we might be looking for.

Rekindle a childhood passion and simplify your search for passions:
1) Describe a childhood passion you enjoyed and whether you would like to rekindle it in an adult context.
2) Describe an activity you've enjoyed as an adult and whether you would like to take it further.

The Influence of our Culture

Our passions can also be influenced by our culture. For example, various sports can have very different followings in countries around the world and this may impact on the sports we choose for ourselves. Another example is the books we read. Through our culture, we can be influenced at a very early age to read certain books, and then through our continuing education we are often directed towards specific books. We might read some of the 'classics', such as Wuthering Heights or Oliver Twist, because our culture has directed us towards those books. We might read something about Feng Shui or Yoga because they've been introduced into our culture. However, unless we're taught to look beyond our literary culture, or unless we choose to actively look beyond it, we can end up restricting ourselves to the literary world that has been pre-defined for us. Instead, we can widen our cultural view and discover many new books. In this way we can expand our potential for finding new passions, and we might also open up new perspectives in our lives.

The opportunity for opening up our literary culture is now greatly assisted by the internet. We can explore the book shelves of the world, look at recommendations from people who have read certain books, and learn about books from numerous countries. We have an amazing opportunity to expand our minds and our cultural view.

Another example of cultural passions are the array of gardening and home decorating programmes around the world, instilling many a passion into the heart of the home owner. These programmes are popular because of the inspiring and original ideas of the designers, and the way they have transformed the idea of interior design and gardening as the 'jobs' that need to be done, into the idea of being fun and entertaining. Such programmes have enabled people to explore a myriad of cultural designs and decorations from around the world.

Widen your cultural view:
1) Find out about other cultures and
    communities in the world. Use the internet,
    read books and articles, talk with others.

2) Learn about the wide variety of sports which are enjoyed in other countries.
3) Take part in a festival that brings different cultures together.

Passionate about a Quality

One of the positive spin offs of being passionate about something is that we can naturally **strengthen qualities** such as determination, motivation, stamina, energy and patience. For example, if we are really passionate about something, then we can apply ourselves with energy and enthusiasm and be determined to succeed, even if we have to push through any mental or physical barriers. So by working with our passions, and taking ourselves through the rough and the smooth, we can strengthen our qualities of energy, enthusiasm, and determination and many other similar qualities. This can serve us well for our current and future passions, and it can also assist us in **strengthening our character** and other areas of our lives.

If we take a slight 'twist' on this, we can say that as well as our passions being able to strengthen various qualities in our minds, we can also *choose* to be passionate about a particular quality. This is very useful information because we can learn to strengthen or exercise a particular quality in our minds simply be being passionate about it. Let me explain: If one person has a passion to 'succeed' in whatever they do, they will strive to overcome any obstacle because of their passion. They might have many difficulties and challenges along the way, but because they have a passion to succeed, they will choose this quality in their minds and motivate themselves to succeed. This doesn't mean this person is devoid of failure. Not everything is going to run according to plan, and sometimes things are outside of their control anyway. However, the *passion* for success always stays with this person, and they choose to use their failures in a positive way by recognising their unique value as opportunities for learning and growing.

Having a passion for a quality, then, is about strengthening our minds so that we can take ourselves through the difficult times as well as the good. If we strengthen and exercise the qualities we value, then we can 'draw' on them when we need.

Here are a few more qualities we can choose to be passionate about: Achievement, Optimism, Originality, Courage, Enjoyment, Self-belief, Sharing, Independence.

Strengthen your qualities:
1) Have a think about some of the qualities you would like to strengthen in your character.
2) Choose to strengthen one of the qualities you've identified by keeping it prominent in your mind and by instilling a sense of passion.
3) Over the next few weeks, strengthen some of

the other qualities you identified. Take some time to think about each of the qualities and what they really mean to you, and then heighten your passion for each of those qualities.

PROFILE OF INTERESTS AND PASSIONS

Having gained an understanding of what passions can really mean in our lives, we now move on to our Profile of Interests and Passions. The purpose is to provide you with a sense of direction for discovering your interests and passions, and you can do this in part be re-visiting your memories. The main idea is to encourage and prompt you to disclose the variety of interests and passions you've had in your life. You will then have a basis for considering interests and passions for pursuing in the present and future.

In compiling your Profile, you will be assisted with various **Prompters**, and these are categorised under a range of different themes. You may want to involve a family member or friend because this can help you to trigger your memories and expand some of your thoughts. Getting a large group of friends together can also work well because you can keep triggering ideas from each other, and you'll be amazed at what you find out about yourself.

CHILDHOOD MEMORIES

What you loved as a child

Have a look at the Prompters below and think about what you loved as a child. A good way to jog your memory is to visualise a place you remember fondly and then think about what you enjoyed there.

This exercise is about rekindling part of what you feel when you 'love' something, since this is a key element of what passions are all about. You can also see more clearly the simplicity of some of the things you loved as a child.

Prompters

Places: Watching boats on the river; going to the beach; picking strawberries on a farm; going to a theme park.

Objects: Eating sweets; playing games; toys.

Activities: Football, tennis, baseball, skating, cycling, cooking, painting, karate, cricket, swimming.

Nature: Climbing the 'character' trees, the ones with the most branches and foot holds; planting a few herbs; feeling the textures of some of the plants in the garden.
Noticing colourful flowers; watching the birds on the lawn.

Nurture: Caring for a pet; trying to feed some rabbits; planting a peach stone and watching it grow into a small peach tree; growing mustard and cress.

How did you feel?

Think about how you felt when you were engaged in your childhood interests. Return to the memories of the places you remember fondly as a child, and then ask yourself some of the questions below:

"Where am I?...Am I outside or inside?"
"What am I doing...Am I reading?...Am I making something?"
"How do I feel?...Am I engrossed?...Am I content?"
"Do I feel frustrated?...Am I impatient?"

TEENAGE MEMORIES

What were your passions as a teenager?

Conjure up some images in your mind and imagine yourself as a teenager. Think about what you really enjoyed. Were you with friends? Did you create something? Perhaps you had a passion for sport.

Additional Prompters

Culture: Subjects at school; cooking; music; reading; playing football.

Curiosity: Asian cooking, meditation, art and design from around the world.

Career: To be a......musician, writer, presenter, nurse, fashion designer.

ADULT MEMORIES

What interests have you loved as an adult?

Think about those activities you've loved as an adult. Again, you can conjure up places in your mind to help you remember.

Additional Prompters

History: Medieval period and its costumes, food, literature, and music.

Music: Writing the lyrics to a song; performing in a musical.

Health: Natural health remedies, reflexology, massage, meditation, yoga.

Entertainment:
Acting, singing, stage design, costumes, make-up, film, sound.

Learning from your Profile

You should now be more aware of the many different types of interests and passions you've had in your life, and the way they have changed and evolved over time. You should be more aware of the different types of emotion that can be attached to your passions, and the 'qualities' you can derive (such as energy and confidence). And you may have collected some ideas about widening your cultural view in your search for new interests and passions. By focusing specifically on your past interests and passions, you can heighten your level of awareness and give yourself a greater opportunity for finding them in the present.

So over the next few days and weeks, you may start remembering even more about your interests and passions because you've activated and exercised that area of your mind. As new ideas arrive, you can add them to your Profile. And remember, your interests and passions serve as a fuel for your life. Spending time with them will enable you to invigorate your life and the lives of others around you.

Key Points

Stress can affect our ability to see our passions. We need to learn to manage what worries us and organise our lives. We need to convert 'problems' into challenges and goals.

Repeating negative mental phrases can 'block' our minds. We have to turn around our negative mental phrases and make them into positive phrases.

We can sometimes single down all of our concerns into just one issue (lumping everything into one basket) without understanding and assessing the individual components. We need to identify our concerns, and then choose our options for moving forwards.

Key Points

We might discover that our work is a self-fulfilling passion, in which case, we need to start searching for new passions outside of work.

We shouldn't be concerned about finding <u>One</u> spectacular passion, but enjoy all of our passions as they arrive in our lives.

> We <u>like</u> our interests, but we <u>love</u> our passions.
>
> We can self-energise with our passions.
>
> Spending time with our interests and passions can invigorate our minds and emotions and increase our sense of well-being.
>
> Our passions can take us through many emotional ups and downs.
>
> Our senses can be a 'by-product' of our passions, or they can be part of what 'fuels' our passions.

We need to simplify our initial search for passions and look at some of our everyday enjoyments.

Reviewing our childhood passions can give us the opportunity to rekindle some of them.

We need to be aware of the way our culture can affect our passions and consider widening our cultural view.

Key Points

Our passions enable us to naturally strengthen qualities such as patience, determination, and stamina.

We can be passionate about a quality, such as 'success', and use our quality to strengthen our minds and our character.

Our Profile of Interests and Passions can provide us with a sense of direction for future interests and passions.

CHAPTER 3   INSPIRATION ACCESSORY

*The stimulation of our thoughts and feelings
that may additionally lead us to some special activity*

Inspiration is about the stimulation of our thoughts and feelings beyond our normal levels. Our emotions rise, our interest accentuates, and even our senses can become more alert and more acute. We can be inspired by a painting....by the emotional experience of music....or by the journey through a thought provoking book. We can be inspired by an inspirational leader....by someone who takes a stand against injustice....or by someone who has struggled against the odds. We can be inspired by a movie and its ability to take us through a range of emotions, or a story of courage that inspires us to achieve greater things in our lives. An artist may be inspired by a love of nature. A poet may be inspired by the nature of 'love' itself.

Of course, the funny thing about inspiration is that like our passions, it can often feel very elusive in our lives. It can also feel very much like a quality that we have to wait for. So we might continue with our normal routine and wait for inspiration to arrive in our lives. But this is where our Inspiration Accessory becomes useful, because it can teach us to *look* for inspiration, and to be an active participant in the life of inspiration.

Now…let's pause a moment…and take some time to consider the following:

> When you are inspired by something, do you ask yourself questions such as "Why does this inspire me?" "What do I feel?" "Am I inspired to actively change my life?" "Can I use aspects of my inspiration to produce something creative?"

Coming up with questions such as those above, and responding to them, is where our Inspiration Accessory has a key role to play. By understanding more about our Accessory, we can learn to contemplate our sources of inspiration at a deeper level, we can learn to see things around us in a different way, and we can broaden the world around us. We can also begin to consider our emotions and senses in relation to our sources of inspiration.

So we know that inspiration can be a great source of energy and pleasure in our lives and that it's worthwhile trying to find it. When we learn about our Inspiration Accessory, and how we can apply it, we can make inspiration a much bigger part of our lives.

What Will I Learn?

You will discover some of the diversities from where inspiration can arise, and why inspiration might be elusive in your life. You will be encouraged to raise your levels of curiosity, and to 'taste' different subjects. You will also learn about the different feelings that inspiration can provide, and how you can raise your levels of awareness of those feelings.

The next stage is about different ways of finding inspiration and learning how to 'open your eyes' to the various inspirational sources around you. You will learn about the 'eight identifiable choices' for applying inspiration, and by being more aware of these choices, you will have the potential to take your inspiration much further. And you will learn about different inspirational sources of the past, and how these sources can be pieced together to form an 'Inspirational Record'.

SOURCES OF INSPIRATION

I've already mentioned that inspiration can derive from many different sources, including paintings, music, literature, and people. We might be inspired by the paintings of Constable or by the surrealist works of Picasso. We might be inspired by classical music or by contemporary artists. We might be inspired by a real life story or by a fictional tale. And when it comes to the people who inspire us, they could be family, friends, teachers, co-workers, celebrities, athletes, singers, and so on. Basically, it can be anyone we are aware of in our lives who inspires us. So all of these different **facets of our lives** provide us with enormous opportunities to gain many different sources of inspiration.

It's clear, then, that the sources of inspiration in our lives can be numerous, so it's probably quite surprising to discover that inspiration can be quite **elusive** in our lives. This elusiveness is partly to do with the way we wrap ourselves in our **routine**, to the point where we don't have the time, or the inclination, to see the sources of inspiration around us. **Stress** also has a way of restricting our inspiration. Just as our passions can become subdued by continuous stress, our inspiration can also become subdued. High levels of stress certainly have a way of 'numbing' different areas of our minds, and if we constantly feel 'knotted' with worry, then we can end up passing by our inspirational sources.

Now, just imagine for a moment that you're trying to find a missing bottle of sauce for a burger you're about to eat....you hunt high and low in the kitchen, searching in every cupboard, on every shelf, in the fridge, and on the bench tops....you even check in the cooker for good measure....but you still can't find the bottle of sauce. You sit down at your kitchen table feeling a little annoyed at having to eat your burger without any flavouring. You know that bottle is around somewhere. And just as you bite into that dry texture of burger and bread, you look up from your plate, and in front of you, there it is. The sauce bottle was on the kitchen table all the time, starring you right in the face! This very sauce bottle is like a metaphor for our inspiration, it's there all the time, but if our minds are too busy thinking about other things, and distracted by routine and worries, then it's going to be more difficult for us to *see* our inspiration.

If we want to allow inspiration to become stronger in our lives, then we need to be much more **receptive** to the sources of inspiration around us. This means reducing any high levels of stress in our lives, and introducing new thoughts and ideas to **break the pattern** of our routine. One way of breaking the pattern is to give our minds a 'taste' of different subjects, and to become more aware of the topics which interest us, or which we are curious about. We can follow up on our subjects and choose to research them by looking for books and videos, or actively get involved in our subjects by joining clubs and organisations. Another way of breaking the pattern is to give ourselves a mental holiday, where we take a break from the normal pattern of our lives. For example, we could take a mental holiday in our own home and choose to sit quietly for a few moments as we contemplate what really interests us. The aim is to allow our minds to move away from our usual thought patterns, and to lead us into new areas of our minds, as we discover new subjects and open up new thoughts, questions, and ideas.

Inspiration Accessory

BITE SIZE TASTERS

The idea of 'Bite Size Tasters' is to raise your interest about various subjects, and to prompt you to 'taste' those subjects, that is, to find out something about them that you didn't already know. You can then choose whether you want to follow them up, or move on to another Bite Size Taster. This gives you a whole range of possibilities, because you don't have to learn about a subject in depth, you can just choose to research a small part, and then see if it grabs your interest.

By deliberately exploring different subjects, we can gain many different benefits. We can learn to open our minds to potential new interests, we can begin to break the pattern of our routine, and we can learn to **raise our levels of curiosity**. Having a curious mind is important for discovering new inspirational sources. Through our everyday living, we can tend to limit our levels of curiosity to the world we know, the world we have defined for ourselves. So in considering all of the above benefits, we can acknowledge that Bite Size Tasters can provide us with a strong foundation for inspirational sources to emerge.

In the following section you will find suggestions, and a few examples, for discovering more about paintings, sculpture, glass, literature, and poetry. You can extend this list with subjects of your own choosing, and think about what your suggestions might be for finding out more about them.

Discover an inspiring painting

Choose a day to visit a public art gallery, exhibition, or private gallery, and look for a painting that inspires you. Think about what inspires you about the painting. Have a look at the colours, the texture, the transparency (if it's a watercolour), the style, the subject, and so on. What emotions do you feel about the painting? Does the painting remind you of a memory?

You can keep asking yourself questions about your painting to try to understand what inspires you.

Review a piece of sculpture

While you're at the gallery, you may come across some pieces of sculpture. Try to find a piece that interests you, and consciously become aware of your thoughts. Again, you can ask yourself some questions about the sculpture to stimulate your thoughts further.

This exercise is about a piece of sculpture that is of 'interest' to you, but not necessarily a piece that inspires you. You might discover, however, that as you unravel your thoughts, your 'interesting' sculpture actually does become inspiring to you.

Discover the variations in glass

Next time you go shopping, have a look at some of the products made from glass, such as ornaments, vases, and trinkets. Note the different styles, colours, shapes, and textures. Think about the craftsmanship that produced those objects. Ask yourself some questions about what you see, and give yourself a few moments.

Literature

When I read some of my favourite classic novels, I find myself inspired by the imagination of the authors, and by their vivid insights into our minds, and especially by the words that somehow transcend themselves through time, to be so very real and relevant to us today. I marvel at the number of eyes that must have read the very same words I find myself reading, and I think about the context in which the books were first read. What were the interpretations of those readers? Were certain novels regarded as challenging in their day? How did certain novels affect people's lives? So we can be inspired by the skill of an author, by their writing style, and by the way their words may have impacted on society, and we can also be inspired by the seemingly timeless nature of their words.

Review a piece of literature

Check the internet, a library, bookstore, or market stall, and explore the possibilities in literature. Have a look through some of the books available and get a 'taste' of what they're about.

To get you started, here is an extract from the classic novel 'Our Mutual Friend' by Charles Dickens:

"It was a foggy day in London, and the fog was heavy and dark. Animate London, with smarting eyes and irritated lungs, was blinking, wheezing, and choking; inanimate London was a sooty spectre, divided in purpose between being visible and invisible, and so being wholly neither. Gaslights flared in the shops with a haggard and unblest air, as knowing themselves to be night-creatures that had no business abroad under the sun; while the sun itself, when it was for a few moments dimly indicated through circling eddies of fog, showed as if it had gone out, and were collapsing flat and cold. Even in the surrounding country it was a foggy day, but there the fog was grey, whereas in London it was, at about the boundary line, dark yellow, and a little within it brown, and then browner, and then browner, until at the heart of the City – which call Saint Mary Axe – it was rusty-black. From any point of the high ridge of land northward, it might have been discerned that the loftiest buildings made an occasional struggle to get their heads above the foggy sea, and especially that the great dome of Saint Paul's seemed to die hard; but this was not perceivable in the streets at their feet, where the whole metropolis was a heap of vapour charged with muffled sound of wheels, and enfolding a gigantic catarrh.

At nine o'clock on such a morning, the place of business of Pubsey and Co. was not the liveliest object even in Saint Mary Axe – which is not a very lively spot – with a sobbing gaslight in the counting-house window, and a burglarious stream of fog creeping in to strangle it through the keyhole of the main door. But the light went out, and the main door opened, and Riah came forth with a bag under his arm.

Almost in the act of coming out at the door, Riah went into the fog, and was lost to the eyes of Saint Mary Axe. But the eyes of this history can follow him westward, by Cornhill, Cheapside, Fleet Street, and the Strand, to Piccadilly and the Albany. Thither he went at his grave and measured pace, staff in hand, skirt at heel; and more than one head, turning to look back at his venerable figure already lost in the mist, supposed it to be some ordinary figure indistinctly seen, which fancy and the fog had worked into that passing likeness.

Arrived at the house in which his master's chambers were on the second floor, Riah proceeded up the stairs, and paused at Fascination Fledgeby's door. Making free with neither bell nor knocker, he struck upon the door with the top of his staff, and, having listened, sat down on the threshold. It was characteristic of his habitual submission, that he sat down on the raw dark staircase, as many of his ancestors had probably sat down in dungeons, taking what befell him as it might befall.

After a time, when he had grown so cold as to be fain to blow upon his fingers, he arose and knocked with his staff again, and listened again, and again sat down to wait. Thrice he repeated these actions before his listening ears were greeted by the voice of Fledgeby, calling from his bed, 'Hold your row! – I'll come and open the door directly!' But in lieu of coming directly, he fell into a sweet sleep for some quarter of an hour more, during which added interval Riah sat upon the stairs and waited with perfect patience.

At length the door stood open, and Mr. Fledgeby's retreating drapery plunged into bed again. Following it at a respectful distance, Riah passed into the bed-chamber, where a fire had been some time lighted, and was burning briskly.

'Why, what time of night do you mean to call it?' inquired Fledgeby, turning away beneath the clothes and presenting a comfortable rampart of shoulder to the chilled figure of the old man.

'Sir, it is full half-past ten in the morning.'

'The deuce it is! Then it must be precious foggy?'

'Very foggy, sir.'

'And raw, then?'

'Chill and bitter,' said Riah, drawing out a handkerchief, and wiping the moisture from his beard and long grey hair as he stood on the verge of the rug, with his eyes on the acceptable fire.

With a plunge of enjoyment, Fledgeby settled himself afresh.

'Any snow, or sleet, or slush, or anything of that sort?' he asked.

'No, sir, no. Not quite so bad as that. The streets are pretty clean.'

'You needn't brag about it,' returned Fledgeby, disappointed in his desire to heighten the contrast between his bed and the streets. 'But you're always bragging about something. Got the books there?' "

Poetry

Poetry has an artistry of its very own. It has a way of stirring up our thoughts and emotions in a different way to the words of novels or other forms of literature. Poetry has the potential to be very powerful, since in just a few words, we can begin to see the world in a different way, or find hidden depths within ourselves. We can also find ourselves puzzling over certain verses when they are shrouded with metaphors and inferences. Only time and dedication can provide us with the full depth of meaning intended.

There are many variations in poetry. They can be subtle, brutal, funny, in your face, romantic…and so on. Some forms of poetry can be very focused, for example, twenty lines might describe just one thing, be it a quality, such as happiness, or an object, such as glass. Some people love certain pieces of poetry so much that they learn them off by heart, treasuring each poem like a precious jewel.

Review a piece of poetry

Check the internet, a library, bookstore, or market stall, and look for some poetry. There are so many different styles of poetry around, with different subjects, thoughts, poetry patterns, styles, etc. Choose a poem of particular interest, and then think about the qualities that attract you to that poem. Is it gentle and calming? Is it observational about life? Does it draw on your emotions? Here are a few examples for you to consider (you can refer to endnotes [3] and [4] for details about the poems):

I Paint a Picture of You

I paint a picture in my mind,
With thoughts on canvas as I find;
Words evolve,
Emotions run,
My mental picture is then begun.

Around the world your portrait shows,
Conveying a message to all that glows;
Fame and splendour,
Glitz and glamour,
My painting sways with the media banner.

But when your words are spoken true,
This is when I see in you,
Behind the glitz,
Beyond the glimmer,
Your portrait now a radiant shimmer.

As more reveals your growing mind,
I see there is much more to find;
Thoughts are spoken,
Feelings awoken,
Directions taking a different kind.

As words engage my portrait new,
I strengthen the textures in my view;
I brighten the colours,
I broaden the canvas,
I feel the nature of what is true.

I can but admire you from afar,
And inspire my mind with who you are;
My dreams are fuelled,
My thoughts arrive,
Once more my painting comes alive.

* * * * * *

The Alfresco Painting

A stranger walked into a gallery one day,
To seek out a painting to inspire in some way,
As they wandered around and absorbed what they saw,
They found the painting they were looking for.

It was light, it was bright,
It was oranges and yellows,
There was movement and talking,
Sitting and walking.

Tables and chairs set out in the sun,
Adorning the pavements, adoring the fun,
Here was the scene of alfresco taste,
Of leisure and pleasure, none in great haste.

Inspiration Accessory

This painting of shops abundant with cakes,
Delectable pastries and other good bakes,
Beguiled the locals and visitors too,
Who resting on seats could admire the view.

Shop fronts with awnings to guard from the sun,
Glass to show off what could be won,
Apartments above of glorious blue,
With other facades of a different hue.

Pavements which sparkled of orange and gold,
White painted chairs which looked rather old,
Tables embellished with flowers and lace,
Each had their role in this wondrous place.

Patrons who put down their bags and thoughts,
Now considered what could be bought,
Would it be savoury? Would it be sweet?
Could they indulge in some special treat?

The eye of the viewer with intrigue did stay,
To study a painting of others at play,
Until the time for departure did come,
The gallery closing to a quietened hum.

Feet who's searching for open doors,
Would return to life and its little chores,
The painting to inspire another day,
Enticing the thoughts of others to stay.

Time – You're Always There

Hello Time, my friend and foe,
You're always there, determined to show,
Through thick and thin you stay in touch,
Leading the way when moments are such
That I need some space to reflect and think,
To move my life to the next new link.

You give me moments for memories to store,
To enjoy and saver, and be wanting more;
But then frustration and annoyance creeps in,
When plans are altered and deadlines stalled,
Time keeps moving with choices to make,
Awaiting ideas for answers to shape.

And in other moments my patience is tried,
Like queuing for tickets, or waiting reply,
Waiting, waiting, for Time to move,
You slowly plod and challenge my mood.

The other day you were sluggish in pace:

"Time – how you move so slow,
As I sit, I watch your hand; it hardly moves.
I'm in this boring lecture…sooo boring,
So I 'will' your hand to move on fast,
To escape this wasted moment past,
To return to 'my time' in the world I know,
Not to sit in frustration and dull my mind."

Inspiration Accessory

Time moves slowly, Time moves quickly.

Last week I made a sculpture new,
I remember then how Time just flew:

"Today, Time, you raced on by,
One hour like a minute, I couldn't keep up,
And enjoying my space I worked on through,
Till daylight hours had all but gone;
Contented still, I carried on,
Till mind and eyes felt tired and long."

At times I see you in the night,
Through hazy eyes and a greyish light,
By my side you give me rest,
Relaxing thoughts to feel my best,
But restless nights, no help at all,
Tossing and turning you completely bore,
Reminding me of sleep that's lost,
And later, Time, you'll be at my cost.

For now I return by your side,
As I see your fame spread far and wide,
You ebb and flow just like the tide,
As each new day you plan your stride;
Sun goes up…..sun goes down,
Buildings rise…..buildings fall,
Cities grow…..cities slow;
Make Time, plan Time,
No Time, out of Time.

THE RESONANCE OF INSPIRATION

'Resonance' can be described as 'echoing, resounding' but it can also mean 'full, rich, and vibrant'. I have used the term 'resonance' to combine with inspiration because when we are inspired by something, it can literally echo in our minds. It can have a real impact in our lives, and it can reverberate in our minds, sometimes for years to come. When we are inspired, it's a similar feeling to being passionate, because in both cases the intensity of our emotions rise, our senses become more acute, and our interest accentuates. But the key difference between being passionate and being inspired, is that our inspiration additionally provides us with the opportunity **to stimulate and generate ideas.**

Our **emotions** are strongly attached to our sources of inspiration, and they can cause us to **focus** more intently on the details. Our minds can bring about feelings such as admiration, surprise, shock, intrigue, and we can often remember the feelings we attach to particular sources of inspiration. Then there are our senses. Our minds can become much more aware of our senses of sight, sound, smell, touch, and taste (although not all of our senses may be involved), and they can help us to absorb more of the detail around us. This heightened level of awareness, through our emotions and senses, combined with the fact that we are likely to use a heightened level of **concentration**, enables us to register a much broader range of details.

If it is a person who inspires us, then we are likely

to pay close attention to the words they say, and potentially find those words more compelling than if we heard them from someone else. If we are inspired by an object, then we are likely to concentrate on the details and to find these much more vibrant and interesting than anything else around us. As our awareness increases, and our interest accentuates, we can become **oblivious** to other things around us. We concentrate heavily on what inspires us.

With the resonance of our emotions, senses, and accentuated interest, we begin to stimulate our minds in a different way. Various questions may cross our minds, new thoughts may be introduced, and different ideas might begin to surface. Thinking 'through' inspiration allows us to enter a different realm of thought, because our inspiration often provides us with new information, and it allows us to uncover in our minds the area that stimulates our **fascination**, something which is individual to all of us, and which helps us to be curious.

Of course, not all of our sources of inspiration will resonate in our minds because it depends on the **degree** on which they **impact** on our minds. If we only feel a slight sense of inspiration, then we might not even give it a second thought. However, if we feel a strong sense of inspiration, we are likely to remember it, at least in the short term if not further down the line. If we 'act' on that strong sense of inspiration, then we are likely to remember it even more, because now we have something to **connect** with our source of inspiration.

In an attempt to recreate a source of inspiration, and to illustrate how it might influence our emotions, senses, and concentration levels, I have put together a short story:

Inspiration at the Theatre

My friend and I were ushered to our places in the theatre and we took our seats near the front of the stage. It was an old theatre, a cosy theatre, with two tiers of semi-circular seating (upper and lower), and private balcony boxes to the left and the right. It had such a sense of character and history, simulating the passage of time of so many famous actors who had performed over the years. I noticed the detailing around the upper tier seating. There were embossed blue and pink flowers with gold outlines, scroll-like leaves of gold and cream, and other decorative details. The ceiling also had its own decoration, with much larger flowers and leaves, and again the use of blues, pinks, gold, and cream.

As I looked around the theatre, I noticed some of the people in the lower tier. Some were well dressed, while others were more casual. I looked up at one of the private boxes and noticed a couple sharing an ice-cream. I was aware of the murmuring of the audience as they settled themselves down, or talked about what they had done in the day. Somehow, the whole room seemed to take on a certain kind of magic. It had a sort of brilliance to it, a glow all of its own.

Before the performance began, some modern music played in the background – or I should say 'mid-ground' because it was sufficiently loud to cause people to raise their voices from a confidential whisper to an audible discussion. I became aware of the contrast between the modern music and the historical old theatre. The music began to build my feelings of anticipation…..my stomach jumped, my heart beat faster, and my breath drew shorter…..now I was ready for the curtains to open.

As the lights turned low, and the crowd quietened, I waited in the silence of darkness…..then suddenly, the spotlight ignited, and the play commenced. I listened intently and became attracted to the storyline, to its surprises, shocks, and humour, and to each new character as they entered the scene. I listened to the different accents and tones of the actors, their expressive movements and calculated expressions. Sometimes the actors would bring the audience back to reality and interact with them, asking rhetorical questions, or stating something humorous as a point of fact.

My mind continued to create an imprint of

my thoughts and feelings, and etched them strongly in my memory. I felt energised and alive as I followed the story, and joined with the audience as we laughed or sighed.

When the curtains closed on the final scene, my thoughts and feelings were still engaged. I stood with the audience to applaud the actors, and after their second bow, it was time to farewell this wonderful experience.

We can consciously and subconsciously record the details of a strong source of inspiration. And we can find ourselves absorbing other information around us if this adds to our inspirational source. An experience such as 'Inspiration at the Theatre' can potentially resonate in our minds for years to come.

Tangible and Intangible

We now come to a very interesting aspect of inspiration, this being that our sources of inspiration can either be tangible or intangible. **Tangible** sources of inspiration are those that retain a **physical presence**, such as a treasured brooch or vase. **Intangible** sources of inspiration are those that we can **physically experience** for a certain period of time, but which remain as a memory, unless we can reignite them again. The experience of 'Inspiration at Theatre' is an example of an intangible source of inspiration which became a memory. Listening to inspirational music is an example of an intangible source of inspiration. We can't hold music in our hands and touch it, but we *can* reignite the experience by listening to it. We can sing it, hum out loud, or play it over in our minds and attempt to reignite that inspirational feeling.

The problem with tangible sources of inspiration is that we don't always appreciate them, and this is partly because they have a physical presence. We can say to ourselves that our inspirational source will be there tomorrow, and the next day, and the next day, so we can appreciate it another time, when we're ready. But if we don't take the time to appreciate tangible sources of inspiration when we find them, we can potentially forget them completely, and continue to lose ourselves in the busy milieu of our world. It's important, then, to take '**time out**' to really consider our tangible sources of inspiration.

The problem with intangible sources of inspiration is that they can fade into the background unless we find ways to **keep them alive in our minds**, such as writing down the atmosphere of a place, remembering what inspired us the most, reflecting on the way we felt, or replaying a piece of music that inspires us.

Record a tangible and intangible source of inspiration:
1) Think about some of your tangible sources of inspiration, or go and look for something.

Once you have your tangible source of inspiration, take some time to describe it, and record the *details* that inspire you the most.

2) Now have a think about an intangible source of inspiration. Maybe it's a play you went to, a musical performance, or a verbal presentation by an inspiring person. Once you have your intangible source of inspiration, take some time to describe it, and record the *qualities* that inspire you the most.

CREATING

If we are to be creative in our lives, then inspiration has a key role to play, because it can **illuminate our thoughts** and give us a **stimulus for new ideas**. 'Creativity' as such covers a broad range of subjects, including the more obvious pursuits of painting, sculpture, music and writing, and maybe the not so obvious pursuits of engineering, maths, and physics. When we create something, we bring it into existence. It might be something we can physically touch, such as Velcro, or something non-physical where our minds have to comprehend the creation, such as a formula to calculate the area of a circle (πr^2). Whatever the creation may be, inspiration is a very useful tool for progressing our thoughts and **evolving our ideas**.

Because inspiration is so important for creativity, it's necessary for many creative people to **look for inspiration** rather than wait for it to arrive. Artists that paint, for example, actively look for inspiration as a way of starting a new picture:

Some artists work outdoors to find inspiration in the 'mood' of a landscape – such as the colours of a scene, the essence of a sky, the topography of land, or the character of different trees.

Other artists are inspired by a **closer view** of nature – such as the colour, texture, and interlacing of different flowers; the tonal variations on a single leaf; or the secretive wildlife of a small enclosure.

Some artists find inspiration in the studio – such as in the display of beautifully shaped objects, luminous glassware, colourful and exuberant fabrics, delicious fruits, or intricately patterned plates.

Some artists find inspiration by viewing other artists work – such as trying to understand the methods used in a particular painting, and by looking at the different techniques and attempting to **experiment** with them.

So the artist can actively look for inspiration and become acutely aware of those things which inspire them the most.

Another way in which certain artists attempt to look for inspiration is by painting '**from the outside in**', that is, they start their painting without any preconceived plan and commence by splashing colours on canvas. Once they are inspired by the shapes of colour they've created, only then do they begin to define how their picture might take its form. Sometimes their paintings might resemble a recognisable picture, other times they might be quite obscure. Jackson Pollack (1912 to 1956) was an American artist who derived inspiration from the paint itself. He would squeeze paint straight out of the tube and onto the canvas, in a sort of 'drip and splash' style.

Architecture is another art which uses abundant sources of inspiration. An architect might draw inspiration from the past, and use the style of Ancient Greek columns for a grand front porch. Another architect might be inspired by the development of new materials, and develop vast areas of wall to wall glass. When an architect attempts to bring something new to the environment, they can seek inspiration from the **past, present and future.** They can look for ways to express and construct futuristic concepts, as well as re-utilise styles from the past and present.

If we now consider the 'inventors', we can again see how inspiration has a key role to play. Inventors can be **inspired by what exists** and adapt or progress it in some way (such as the progression of the landline phone to the mobile phone), and they can also be **inspired by what doesn't exist**, that is, they can be inspired to create something which is entirely new (such as the Velcro example). Velcro was discovered in 1948 by Georges de Mestral, a Swiss engineer. It all began through his **curiosity** over the 'burrs' which clung to him and his dog when they were out in the fields. He began to wonder exactly how these burrs were able to cling to his dog, and to certain items of clothing. When he looked at a burr under a microscope, he noticed that they were made up of tiny hooks, and that each of these hooks could easily attach themselves to hair, or to any cloth which was made up of threads. He decided that a man-made version of a burr would be a very useful replacement for buttons and other fastenings, and hence Velcro was created. Velcro has of course progressed from its original use in clothing to a huge variety of applications.

When it comes to the creation of a formula, it's interesting to consider some of the different sources of inspiration which have triggered people's thoughts. One of the most memorable sources of inspiration has to be when Sir Isaac Newton (1642-1727) watched an apple fall to the ground. He suddenly had the idea that the force that controlled the apple was the same force that controlled the motion of the moon. He was inspired to take this further through several experiments, including calculating the force required to pull an object to the ground, and among the formulas he eventually produced was 'F = MA', meaning that Force is the product of Mass multiplied by Acceleration. Through subsequent investigations he was able to calculate the force which was required to hold the moon in its orbit, and he identified this fundamental force as 'gravitation'. Newton was inspired by the **desire to understand** how the universe functioned, and why things were the way they were. He wanted to **discover the unknown**.

The creation of another type of formula was the Pythagoras Theorem, developed by the Greek mathematician and philosopher Pythagoras (c.582 – c.500 BC). The Theorem states that the square of the hypotenuse of a right-angled triangle is equal to the sum of the squares on the other two sides. By bringing together the measurements of a right angled triangle, and the numbers connected with those measurements, he created the Pythagoras Theorem: $b^2 = a^2 + c^2$. This theorem still stands today and is used as a formula to calculate many different types of mathematical and engineering solutions. One of the main motivations that Pythagoras had for his investigations was the inspiration he derived from **nature and numbers**. He believed there was a unity between the two and that numbers were the language of nature.

In summary, we can say that whatever we create in our lives, inspiration can help us to keep our thoughts alive and to nourish our enthusiasm and energy. If we think like an artist, then we can open our eyes to the world and choose to *look* for inspiration rather than wait for it to arrive. We can take a closer view of the world and choose to *understand* what we see rather than accept what our eyes simply acknowledge. And we can *experiment* with what we know and come up with new ideas and opportunities. We can also think like an architect and look at the past, present, and future, and search for different ways to express the inspiration we find. Finally, we can look at 'what exists' and 'beyond what exists' so that we can develop our inspirational sources and take them in new directions.

The other key aspect as mentioned above is to develop our levels of curiosity. When we nurture our curiosity and the desire to understand, then we can automatically increase our prospects for finding inspiration. As previously explained, this is because curiosity helps us to increase our depth of knowledge for specific subjects, and gain a wider appreciation of the world around us. Taken overall then, when we develop the ability to use our inspiration for creativity, then we can truly open our minds to new opportunities and new experiences, and generate a whole new sense of growth in our lives.

Receptive

Arriving without Looking

I want to mention briefly how inspiration can arrive in our minds even though we haven't been looking for it. An example might be someone who watches a programme on the building of Egyptian pyramids and becomes so inspired that they attempt to make a scale model of one of the pyramids. Another example might be someone who has heard a piece of music for the first time and which they find so inspiring that they write a poem about the music. Having said this, however, one fact needs to be pointed out about inspiration when it 'arrives without looking', and that is, that we still need to be **receptive** to inspiration if we are to register it in our minds. You may recall the metaphor I used about looking for a bottle of sauce for a burger, and how this relates to being receptive to the inspirational sources around us. If we aren't aware of the way inspiration can influence our lives, or if we simply aren't bothered by the way we can use inspiration, then we are likely to pass it by as just another piece of information. We combine it with the ever increasing mass of information that passes across our minds every day. So remember, we need to be *receptive* to inspiration and learn to *register* it in our minds.

Acting on Inspiration

We know that when we are inspired by something we don't always act upon it, maybe because it seems too

disconnected and alien from our lives, or maybe we tell ourselves that we are just **too busy** to think about inspiration. But whatever the reason may be, it's worth examining whether we *can* act upon a particular source of inspiration, because we already know that inspiration can have a very positive impact on our lives.

We don't have to force ourselves to act upon everything that inspires us, we just need to think about how that inspiration might impact on our lives, and whether we want to make a connection. An example might be someone who is inspired by a singer. If they consider what they find inspiring about the singer, then they can come up with some **qualities** and think about how they might incorporate them into their own lives. So, for example, they may identify qualities such as strength of character, determination, success, and the ability to keep striving for new sounds. The person could then incorporate these qualities into their life by developing their own strength of character, becoming more determined to succeed, and by pursuing new ideas to keep moving forwards. Finding the qualities in a person that inspires us can provide us with a **resource to inspire our own lives**.

Another example of something which might inspire could be a beautiful glass ornament in a shop window. The twists in the glass and the multiple colours which run through the glass take you quite by surprise. It's like nothing you've ever seen before. You might decide to treasure this ornament in your mind, or you might decide to buy it, but whether it becomes a treasure in your mind or a treasure in your house, it remains a source of inspiration. It is from this point that you can decide whether your inspirational source will make a connection with your life, or whether you will take pleasure purely from its creation. Having an awareness of the potential for connections allows you to think of some of the **avenues for acting on inspiration**. The possibilities could include representing the ornament on canvas, using it in a short story, or creating your own ornament. Identifying avenues that we can take our inspiration can help us to be creative, as well as help us to see much more than the subject of our inspiration.

In summary, if we want to increase the connections with our inspirational sources, then we need to think more about **acting on inspiration**. Two ways we can do this are to consider the **qualities** which make us feel inspired, or the **avenues** which our inspiration can take us.

People who Inspire

Having mentioned already that people can inspire us, it's worth remembering that these people come from all **different facets of our lives**. They might be people who are close to us, such as family and friends, people who pass through our lives, such as school teachers or work colleagues, or people we can only perceive from a distance, such as world leaders, singers, movie stars, or other people in the public eye. The way they inspire us can be quite varied. Teachers who inspire us might enable us to take our knowledge further. Friends who inspire us might cause us to emulate some of their qualities. Courageous people who inspire us might cause us to be more fearless in our lives.

Because our minds can become so busy with everything we have to do, we can easily lose sight of the people who have inspired us in our lives, and in some instances, we can remain entirely unaware of the qualities that inspire us about a particular person. This is why I want to introduce you to the idea of keeping a **List of Inspirational People**. We can build up our List so that it becomes a resource of the qualities we individually admire and value. We can then retain and grow our List, and keep it as a permanent record of the people who have made a difference in our lives.

As already discussed in 'Acting on inspiration', if we identify the qualities we find inspiring about a particular person, then we can think about how we might use those qualities in our own lives. Compiling a List of Inspirational People can assist us in this process, because we can keep a written record of the qualities that inspire us the most, and by understanding some of the **reasons for our inspiration** we can begin to **understand ourselves better**.

Some of our inspirational people are likely to

change over time, and might even disappear from our inspirational radar, but they're still important to keep on our List, because they are a reflection of the progressive movements of our inspiration. If we *do* change our opinion about a particular person, then we have the option to write down why our inspiration has changed, and again understand more closely how we have moved on in our thoughts. Having our List of Inspirational People can also help to prompt us of the qualities we might want to strive for.

Compile a List of Inspirational People:
Have a think about the people who inspire your life, past and present, and consider the qualities you admire in them. Qualities might include strength of character, ability to motivate, leadership skills, compassion, creative abilities, assertiveness, courage.

Write down at least five people that inspire you and write about the qualities you perceive or know for each person.

An Inspirational Sourcebook

When it comes to acting on our inspirational sources, it's not necessarily something we can do straight away, because we don't necessarily know how we might use a particular source of inspiration. It can also take time for our minds to digest the various ideas we might gain from our inspirational sources. This is where an **Inspirational Sourcebook** comes in handy. An Inspirational Sourcebook is our personal collection of quotes, pictures, ideas, and basically anything we find inspiring. Compiling an Inspirational Sourcebook is a useful way of keeping a permanent record of what inspires us so we can **trigger our inspiration** at a later time. It's important to keep a record of inspiration because we can easily forget what inspires us (unless it's something really outstanding).

The format and content of your Sourcebook is entirely up to you, and the more you personalise it the more it will reflect your individual sources. As you compile it, you will probably notice many more inspiring sources around you because you've raised your awareness of inspiration.

When you record your various sources, remember to write down your thoughts and ideas as they relate to each source, so you can follow them up later. Then, when you have your Inspirational Sourcebook well underway, you will be able to use it as a resource for stimulating and applying your inspiration.

A Selection of Sources

To give you an idea of the many varied inspirational sources that people can have in their lives, here are just a few comments I collected from a random sample of interviews:

Buying a new bed quilt was a source of

inspiration for one person, since it gave them the incentive to redecorate their bedroom, and to use the colours of the quilt as the basis for their colour scheme.

Another person described their garden as a source of inspiration, because it always gave them pleasure to watch the flowers grow, and to marvel at their ability to keep producing wonderful shapes and colours.

Another person was so inspired by their trip to Kenya, that they decided to redecorate their lounge with a safari type feel, including pots of bamboo, wooden sculptures of giraffes, and elephant ornaments.

Collecting stones on the beach was a source of inspiration for one person. She described how she enjoyed walking along the beach and collecting several stones on the basis of their colour, texture, shape, and pattern. She might pick up a stone that had been rounded over time, and then pick up another stone for its unusual markings. She would marvel at the millions and billions of stones in the world, and yet the stones she held in her hand were one of a kind. There would never be a complete replica of those stones in shape, colour, texture, or markings – not anywhere in the world. This person was also inspired by the symbolism she attached to the stones. She described how the millions of different stones in the world represented the way human beings are all so different, since not one stone is exactly the same, and not one person is exactly the same – each person is an individual.

One of the more unusual sources of inspiration I came across was the response from a woman who stated very confidently "fruit salad!" I wondered what she meant by this, so I enquired some more. She explained that she was inspired when she made a fruit salad because of all the different types of fruit she could use, and the amazing variety of colours, textures, and shapes which could become that fruit salad. Every time she made up a fruit salad, it would always be different. She might leave grapes whole or chop them up, dice some apples or cut them into crescents, use cherries or strawberries for a colour contrast, add some sliced kiwi fruit, cut a banana into long thin slices or chop into circles. She would feel a sense of creativity and happiness whenever she made fruit salad, and she was inspired to create something new each time.

Nature was a source of inspiration for another person, of rolling green fields, hedgerows, wildlife, and wildflowers, and the remarkable way nature could adapt through various seasons.

Another person was inspired by birds, to see

their different colours and distinctive characteristics, to see some of the rarer birds in their back garden, to wonder at the thousands of miles they had to fly, to wonder how some of the tiniest of birds could survive the harshest of weather conditions, and to listen to the range of different sounds they made, such as warning other birds, or singing at their loudest as if to say "I'm the greatest".

APPLYING

When we are inspired by something and want to act upon it, there are many different ways we can apply it. Having said this, however, it *is* possible to identify a clear set of choices for applying our inspiration, and by viewing these choices, we can give ourselves a greater understanding of how we might use a particular source of inspiration. The **eight identifiable choices** are:

1. Find out more about it
2. Copy it using the same medium
3. Adapt it using the same medium
4. Convert it through a different medium
5. Select a particular aspect and convert it through a different medium
6. Combine it with other ideas/ inspirational sources
7. Evolve it
8. Revolutionise it

As well as helping us to choose a method for applying our inspiration, the above eight choices can also help us to open our eyes to those things around us which we might otherwise regard as quite 'ordinary'. By 'ordinary' I mean not only those things which seem purely functional, such as a kettle, but also those things that we become accustomed to, so that we can't see anything inspiring in them anymore, such as the fabric covering on a lounge chair.

We can explore these eight identifiable choices and how they might be applied by considering a specific example. In this instance, we're going to consider an example of a large terracotta pot which has been produced as a decorative ornament. It's about 600mm high (24 inches) and 430mm wide (17 inches), and has embossed details of leaves and flowers:

If we assume we are inspired by this terracotta pot, we can consider each of the eight identifiable choices available to us and examine what we might produce.

1. Find out more about it
We might be inspired to find out some of the history behind these particular shaped pots, and

investigate how the shape came about in the first place. We could research the designs of ancient Egypt and Greece, and look at some of the early Venetian pots. We could discover how some were made for decoration, while others, like amphora's, were used for storing wine or oil and had quite a different shape. We could ask questions such as "why was the pot such a well used shape?" "Did they experiment with other shapes, and if so, why did they abandon them?"

An amphora for holding wine or oil

By finding out more about pots of the past, we might discover some very interesting shapes and patterns, and some of them might again trigger our inspiration. Also, by increasing our knowledge of how the design of our terracotta pot came about, we might come up with some ideas about how to feature it in our garden or home, such as creating an area in our garden with an ancient Greek theme.

2. Copy it using the same medium

We might choose to copy our pot and make a replica out of clay. By moulding our own pot by hand, we can learn much more about the way it was formed, since we have to study it in more detail. We would need to assess the curves of the pot, the shape of the neck, the embossed details, etc.

3. Adapt it using the same medium

A slightly different choice for applying our inspiration would be to adapt our pot, but still using the medium of clay. For example, we could make a range of different sized pots, we could make a few pots just 6cm high and use them as ornaments in the house, we could change the shape and make it slimmer, we could add our own decorative details, we could expand it and create a clay sculpture, or we could use different glazes.

4. Convert it through a different medium

If we choose to convert our pot through a different medium, then we have a much wider range of possibilities. Examples could include creating a mosaic, developing a textile, creating a brooch, making something from glass, or even writing a poem.

 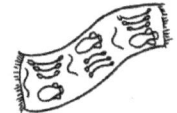 

5. Select a particular aspect and convert it through a different medium

We can choose to select a particular aspect of our pot instead of using the whole shape and decoration. We might select a leaf detail and make a delicate necklace, we could use the flower details and represent them on a silk scarf, or we could use the neck of the pot to create some unusual shaped paperweights.

6. Combine it with other ideas/inspirational sources

We might choose to combine what we find inspiring about our pot with other ideas and/or inspirational sources. Although some of the choices mentioned above already include an element of combining with other mediums (such as the mosaic or use of glass) the reason for identifying 'combine it with other ideas/inspirational sources' is to remind ourselves that we can use *numerous* ideas and inspirational sources to come up with something creative. For example, we could use part of the shape of our pot, combine it with ideas from an inspiring landscape, combine it with a portion of an Italian building, combine it with a fascinating fabric, and come up with our own unique painting as a collection of the inspiring thoughts we gained from our inspirational sources. There are an infinite number of combinations available if we choose to apply this choice.

7. Evolve it

If we choose to evolve our inspirational source, then we can keep coming up with creative ideas and progress one idea on to the next. We won't know where we're going to end up, because that's the whole idea of evolving it. If we think about our inspirational pot, we might choose to initially create some small decorative pots, and then from those pots create a vase, and then from the vase create a painting. Evolving our ideas in this way enables us to end up with a painting that we hadn't initially thought of because it was the result of evolving ideas. So when we apply the choice of 'evolve it' to our inspirational sources, we are specifically thinking about how to progress one idea on to the next and therefore to keep taking our inspiration through a continual evolution.

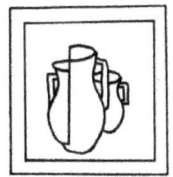

8. Revolutionise it

If we choose to revolutionise our inspirational source, then it's going to be something that's quite different from anything we currently know or have. It means a complete move away from what first inspires us, since revolutionary means something that involves 'great change'. An example of something revolutionary which relates to our inspirational pot is the way the plastics industry has created a wide variety of garden and household pots as a cheaper and lighter alternative to clay pots. Today, it's difficult to tell the difference between a clay pot and a plastic imitation of a clay pot unless we tap them or try to pick them up.

If we were to revolutionise our inspirational pot, we might decide to create a completely new shape, such as a star, or an upside down funnel.

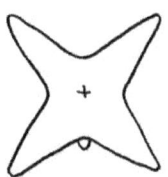 

Whenever we want to choose 'revolutionise it', the key to remember is that we have to know all about our inspirational source, otherwise we might come up with something that's already been developed or discovered. When we know what's already out there, we can attempt to explore completely different and revolutionary ideas. In other words, in knowing the rules we can 'break the rules' and create something new.

While the above eight identifiable choices can be chosen individually, we can also use two or more choices at the same time. So we might choose 'convert it through a different medium' and also choose 'evolve it' as we keep searching for progressively creative ideas. Whether we use our choices individually or grouped, it is for us to decide, and for us to explore.

Apply an inspirational source:
Look around for something that inspires you. It might be the design of a watch, the shape of a leaf, or the sound of a bird. Once you have your inspirational source, have a look at the eight identifiable choices and think about which one you would apply.

INTERPRETING

When we think about applying our inspiration, there is one very important process that needs to occur. We need to think about the way we want to *interpret* our inspiration. One aspect of 'interpreting our inspiration' is about identifying the qualities we are attracted to for a particular source of inspiration (as discussed in 'Acting on Inspiration'). Another aspect involves the way we might interpret our inspiration by applying one or more of the eight identifiable choices, as mentioned above. But another very important aspect of 'interpreting our inspiration' involves the way we choose to **represent** our source of inspiration **at a very detailed level**. For example, we might recognise that the terracotta pot described above is fascinating to us because of its size, shape, colour, and texture, and we might then choose to 'convert it through a different medium' and create a mosaic, but interpretation doesn't stop there. Having already selected one of our eight identifiable choices, we now think about representation at a more detailed level. If we've decided to create a mosaic on a circular outdoor table, we can now start to think about the size of the tiles, the colours, the style of the picture, the mood of the image, etc. So this **third aspect of interpretation** includes our choice of style, and any messages we want to convey in our work, be they transparent or partially hidden.

Another example is about two people who might be inspired by the beauty of a single yellow flower, to look at its colour and form, to touch and feel its texture, to see that flower standing firm and upright on a delicate and thin green stem, and to watch it battle against the wind as it sways back and forth, but somehow always regains its composure, head uplifted, and stem straight up to the sky. The first person might be inspired to capture the essence of that flower by painting a picture to highlight its varying colours and tones, and the finer details of texture and light. The second person might be inspired by the sheer determination of this plant to fulfil its mission…"to flower"…and to stand firm and tall. That same person might see the flower as a metaphor for their own lives, that they too can be determined in their goals and stand tall and resolute against the obstacles that life may throw at them. So we can be inspired by the same thing, but through our *personal interpretation* we can use an inspirational source in our own way.

This 'third aspect' of interpretation can also apply through the same medium, such as a painting. For example, two artists can use their own interpretations when painting a group of red roses. One person might represent the roses through an **abstract** painting of warm colours, including oranges, pinks, and reds, while another might decide to paint the roses as **realistically** as they can, and attempt to capture all of the colours, tones, light, and shade. Both artists use the same medium of paint, but their interpretations are very different. So interpreting our inspiration is very **personal**. Interpretation allows us to show our **individuality,** as well as our ideas, and it allows us to **explore our minds**. When we interpret our inspiration, we carry out the mental thinking that takes us forwards with our ideas.

Having explained how personal interpretation can help us to apply our sources of inspiration, I want to discuss how it can work against us in finding our inspiration. One of the difficulties with personal interpretation is that when we interpret something *before* we are inspired by that 'something', then there is the potential for us to look past what *could* be inspiring. For instance, if we have already made up our minds that a particular painting is a load of rubbish then we won't even remotely consider if there is anything inspiring about it. However, if we become more aware of our 'personal interpretations' then we can actually make it work for us in a positive way because we can question our thoughts and feelings and try to see beyond our normal assumptions to discover another layer of thought. This is how it might work:

Different Interpretations of a Painting

Visualise yourself in an old art gallery, and while you're in the gallery get ready to view three paintings. As you visualise each painting in your mind, think about your interpretations:

The gallery comprises two large rooms linked by a two metre wide archway. Continuous timber floors run throughout the gallery, and black padded benches occupy each of the rooms. White painted walls present their clean canvas on which selected paintings are hung. Several sculptures are also exhibited in each room.

As you enter the gallery, your mind lights up with feelings of expectation... *'will I see something to inspire and stimulate my thoughts?'*

The first painting you view is of a scene by a river bank. In the foreground, a woman is dressed in a cream dress, blue shawl, and cream bonnet. She is sitting at the edge of a river bank feeding a swan on the water. A large tree shades her on this warm summer's day. The river is as smooth as icing on a cake, not even the faintest ripple can be seen. In the background, a large number of trees can be seen, and all of them have a varying shade of green. The largest of the trees begin to show their character as their branches highlight the twists and turns of time.

Exercise 1
Have a think about this painting, what it might mean to you, and any emotions it might conjure. Really visualise it in your mind as you think about your interpretations.

* * * * * *

The second painting is the scene of white water cascading down a rock face, crashing and foaming into the river below. The cascade of water shows a relentless energy and force as it plummets over the rock face. When the cascade finally meets with the river below, huge areas of fine mist dance and spray in the air. Further down the river, the water is more settled, but it still flows with a relentless energy as it reaches ever forward to meet its next destination. You begin to imagine the damp cool air around this place.

You step back to sit on the bench behind you and continue to view the painting. As you sit there, you become more aware of other people milling around the gallery. Many of them pause at the paintings and look at them more closely, while others pass them by, and sometimes with just a glance.

Exercise 2
Have a think about the second painting. Is your interpretation different from the first painting? Does it provide you with any emotions? Is a message being conveyed in the painting?

* * * * * *

Having gathered your thoughts, you stand up and walk over to a third painting. It's another picture of a waterfall, but there's something different about this one. Like the previous painting, it has white water rushing over a rock face and a fine mist and a haze at the bottom of the waterfall, but the most memorable aspect of this painting is not the waterfall…..it's a giant lemon! A giant lemon is perched at the top of the waterfall and is about to cascade over the rock face and into the water below.

As you begin to think about what the artist was trying to convey in the painting, you can sense other people around you who also looking at the image. You listen to some of their comments: *"I don't understand it"… "Why ruin a beautiful scene like that"… "It's one of those modern paintings"… "It's very obscure, I don't like it."*

Exercise 3
As with the previous two exercises, think about this painting and what your interpretations might be. What effect does this painting have in comparison to the others?

* * * * * *

The first painting can be interpreted as a scene of tranquillity and calm as well as the passing of time, as represented by the woman's clothing and the description of the trees. We could take this further if we want to and consider who the woman might be and what period of time she comes from. We could

Interpreting

ask how she's come to be in this place and what she's thinking as she feeds the swan on the river.

The second painting can be interpreted as energetic and vibrant as the artist attempts to capture water as a strong force of nature. We can engage our sense of touch as we imagine the dampness and coolness of the air, and we can remind ourselves that some aspects of nature can make us feel exhilarated, while other aspects can make us feel calm.

When it comes to the third painting, this illustrates how personal interpretations can have the potential to stand in the way of inspiration. The artist may have used the lemon as a metaphor of personal 'taste', such as bitter-sweet, since a couple of the comments from the people viewing the painting are biting, while one is a little sweeter and inquisitive. One of the purposes of this third painting is to promote a **reaction**, so it doesn't matter whether the comments are negative or positive, it will still be achieving one of its aims. Another reason for the painting is to allow people to apply their own interpretations, so there is a direct attempt to get people to *think,* and potentially to **instil inspiration**.

When we come across paintings that are different to those we are used to, our minds have to make an abrupt adjustment, and in so doing, we can invigorate our thinking patterns. If it's something we aren't expecting, then we can start to trigger our minds to think in ways outside of our convention, and allow our minds to come up with new thoughts and ideas.

So rather than dismiss an obscure painting, it's useful to **look behind the first layer of paint** and get underneath some of the meanings that might be conveyed, as well as question what we see. This can then assist us in our search for inspiration.

Back in the art gallery:
You continue to look at some of the other paintings in the art gallery, until it's time for you to go. As you make your way towards the exit, you occasionally hear a few comments about other paintings, and then the voices gradually fade into the distance. You are left to contemplate which of the paintings they were referring to: *'That's an interesting colour, it must be a mixture of blue and purple'… 'The artist has really captured the emotions of that cold and desolate landscape'… 'Those flowers are exquisite'… 'How did the artist capture that sense of tranquillity?'*

RADIAL AND LINEAR

We know at this point that inspiration can come in many different forms and can arrive in many different ways. We've learned how inspiration can derive from a tangible object, such as glass, or from an intangible memory, such as music. We've noted that when inspiration arrives in our minds it might emerge through the active stimulation of our thoughts, or it might purely arrive by chance. And we've learned that we can apply our inspiration through eight identifiable choices and that we can use these as a basis for triggering a variety of creative ideas. So now we come to our final consideration on inspiration, and that is, to explore the concepts of a 'Radial Approach' and a 'Linear Record' as ways of applying our inspiration.

Radial Approach

When we create something from inspiration, an enormous number of thoughts cross our minds; we sort through ideas, we sift through possibilities, and we fine tune the details. We might start with a particular source of inspiration, and then add other ideas and inspirational sources as they emerge along the way. And as we sift through all this information, we begin to make progress towards our creative endeavour.

Sometimes we can have so many ideas and inspirational sources that our minds can feel quite clogged and overloaded. This is where an approach for applying inspiration can be very useful. The concept of a '**Radial Approach**' illustrates the way we can see all our different ideas and inspirational sources as we move towards application and creativity. It's a model for helping us to identify and record our thoughts in relation to a specific project. It's essentially the way we can use one or more sources of inspiration to aid creativity. *Figure 1* shows the principle, with different sources of inspiration on the outer edge of the circle (S), the arrival of inspiration through radial lines, and the application of inspiration at the centre (A).

A Radial Approach is rather like visualising an old wooden cartwheel, with each spoke representing the connection between an inspirational source and the application of that source. The centre represents the application of our inspiration (A) but it can also be seen as a metaphor for our minds, since we are bringing our ideas and inspirational sources into our minds and thinking about them before we produce something creative. Even if there's only one source of inspiration, we're still collecting that source and bringing it into our minds so that we can think about it and decide how to use it for our selected creation.

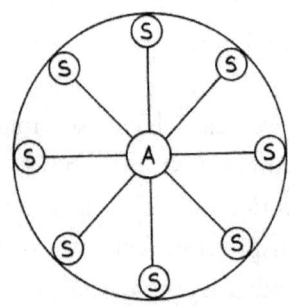

Figure 1
A Radial Approach for applying inspiration
A = Applying inspiration for creativity
S = Source of inspiration

Interpreting

Applying inspiration at the centre of the circle represents the way we can draw inspirational sources and ideas into our minds, and apply our thoughts for creativity. The radial lines represent the way we can find our inspiration: for example, it can arrive by chance, we can seek it out, or we can evolve it.

We often use a Radial Approach instinctively in our minds when we select various sources of inspiration from memory, and then combine them to bring about something creative. It's just that we don't usually see this approach in a conceptual way. Understanding and using a Radial Approach, even though it appears quite simple, can help us with our creative ideas, because we can acknowledge all the sources of inspiration and ideas that might assist us in creating. We can even pick objects and thoughts at random (i.e. they don't have to be inspirational), note them in our Radial Approach, and attempt to come up with something creative.

Using some examples of inspirational sources and ideas, we can utilise our list of 'eight identifiable choices', and combine this with a Radial Approach to illustrate how we can create:

> Imagine you're inspired to create a new form of seating using different materials and different shapes. You want to make a radical change in seating design, and possibly create something revolutionary. The choices you're already considering in your mind are 'combine it with

other ideas/inspirational sources' and 'revolutionise it'.

You decide you want to move from a four legged chair to something quite different, something that can be developed with just a single support to leave more leg room underneath. Other ideas you have are to use a bright red textile for dramatic effect, and to incorporate the shape of a heart. You're inspired by geometric shapes and you experiment with cones to create your chair. You have many other ideas whizzing around in your head as you think about creating your chair.

By using a Radial Approach, you note down your ideas and experiment and refine them as you pursue your goal. You eventually come up with a bright red heart shaped chair, with a central support, and a conical emphasis:

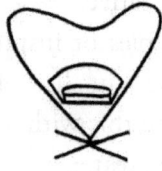

The above heart shaped chair is not a new idea for us today, because it was first developed by Verner Panton in 1959. However, the heart shaped chair was certainly revolutionary in its day, and it made a real impact on the design of chairs that followed. The reason for the above example is to illustrate how we might conceive an idea as we pull together our inspirational sources and thoughts, and how we can relate these to the choices we make for applying our inspiration. So if we learn to think more consciously about what inspires us, we have the opportunity to make something from our inspiration, and we can do this by thinking about our eight identifiable choices, and by using a Radial Approach to refine our creative response.

Linear Record

Our next consideration is the way we can create a **Linear Record** of inspiration by grouping together inspirational sources that are linked in some way. A Linear Record of Inspiration can be defined as something that shows the link between a *source* of inspiration, and the *product* of that inspiration (***Figure 2***). It's rather like visualising a string of pearls, with each pearl representing a source of inspiration, and the last pearl representing a product of inspiration. The last pearl always remains a product of inspiration until that product becomes a source of inspiration that inspires someone to create something else.

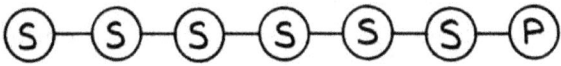

Figure 2
A Linear Record of inspiration
S = Source of inspiration
P = Product of inspiration

A 'link' creates a connection between two sources of inspiration, or between a source of inspiration and the product of that inspiration. A Linear Record of Inspiration might start with a song (Pearl 1), which then inspires someone to write a story (Pearl 2). The story in turn might inspire someone to create a sculpture (Pearl 3), which in turn inspires someone to create a vase (Pearl 4). So the string of Pearls can keep on growing in this way as each Pearl inspires creativity.

The story below provides a more detailed example of the way a Linear Record of Inspiration might occur. The story progresses through a series of scenes in which several people discover something inspiring, and in turn become motivated to produce something creative. It's a clear example of a Linear Record of Inspiration because each pearl is connected to the other.

> A man walks around an art gallery looking at a range of different paintings. As he walks around the gallery, he observes an assortment of qualities and contrasts: bright and subtle colours; busy and quiet depictions; isolated and vibrant landscapes; realistic and impressionistic styles. One painting in particular catches his attention. It's a painting of a woman sitting in a chair in an apartment. She is wearing a cream dress, and is gazing out of her apartment window, searching for something not seen by

the viewer. With the exception of the dress, the painting is represented mainly in sepia shades. She appears to be lost in her own thoughts, but does not reveal any extreme emotion.

*

The man is inspired by the painting, so he decides to capture the essence of the woman in a sculpture, of smooth white alabaster. The statue is small, about ten inches tall, but is minutely detailed, particularly in the features of her face. The statue exhibits an almost luminous quality, of serenity and elegance. It also evokes a sense of mystery through the expression on her face. The statue is eventually put on display in an art gallery.

*

One day, a woman sees the statue and decides to buy it. The statue sits on her mantelpiece for a number of years and many people admire its quality. On one occasion, a young man visiting the house notices the statue and studies it in detail. He is captivated by its quality, and particularly by the face, as it seems to be pondering some hidden thoughts.

The young man is inspired by the statue and decides to write a poem. Some of the verses from the poem read:

Inspiration Accessory

> How I wonder at your thoughts within,
> The mask that wears so smooth;
> The iridescence of serenity,
> And eyes that can but soothe.

The poem is published with a collection of other poems.

*

Some time later, a woman happens to come across the poem and finds inspiration from some of the verses. She decides to write a song representing some of the qualities, and it eventually finds its way onto a record label. The music is heard by millions of people.

*

One day, as the song plays on the radio, a couple listening to the music are struck by the lyrics and the energy of the song. It jolts them out of their routine and makes them begin to think about the direction of their lives and what they want to do next. Over time, they talk over their plans with family and friends, and eventually, they decide to take a totally new direction. They move to France and buy a beautiful Chateau and vineyard. Their dream is to become one of the best wine producers in France.

*

Some time later, a man visits the vineyard as part of a group tour of the area. They are all captivated by the beauty of the Chateau, with its three storeys, two round turrets, white washed walls, and orange window shutters. And on this lovely sunny day in France, the vineyard looks glorious, with its neat rows, welcoming pathways, and abundance of grapes.

The man is so inspired by the Chateau and vineyard that he tries to capture the essence of the place in a painting. He puts paint to canvas and uses an abundance of colour, and through each brush stroke he attempts to capture the splendour and emotions of the place. Several weeks later, the finished painting is found in an art gallery and is seen by numerous people.

*

Later on, a person looking around the art gallery discovers the painting and is inspired by the techniques and brush strokes which capture the essence of the place. The title of the painting is 'Mystical Chateau and Vineyard in France'.

The person studies the painting more closely and tries to understand how the brush strokes have been achieved. As they look more intently, they notice the face of a woman looking out of one of the Chateau windows. She seems to be looking at the distant horizon, lost in thought, but with a sense of serenity and calm.

* * * * * *

The story above illustrates the way a single source of inspiration can become part of a Linear Record of Inspiration. The Pearls in the story are:

Painting – sculpture – poem – song – French Chateau and vineyard – painting

Through a Linear Record, we can **discover sources of inspiration** which were previously unknown to us or have long since been forgotten. We can also **see the progression of different ideas** and learn from the choices that were taken.

So when you next discover something inspiring, have a think about the Linear Record that could be part of your inspiration. You might even think about researching a Linear Record for a specific subject and discover new Pearls of inspiration that might stimulate your mind even further.

CONCLUSION

The magic and diversity of inspiration is open to everyone, we just have to learn to see it, understand our opportunities for using it, and then choose if we want to apply it. When we begin to see inspiration around us more clearly, we can become more aware of those things that we previously considered as 'ordinary' or not important. We can absorb the energy and pleasure that can be derived from inspiration, and we can activate areas of our minds that were previously untouched or unexamined. When you Accessorise your Mind with Inspiration, your world and your opportunities will grow.

Key Points

Inspiration can derive from many different sources and from the many different facets of our lives.

The stress and routine of our lives can restrict our inspiration.

We can learn to be more receptive to inspiration by 'tasting' different subjects.

Raising our levels of curiosity can help us to find inspiration.

> When we're intensely inspired by something, it can literally resonate in our lives.

> The resonance of inspiration can cause our emotions to rise, our senses to become more acute, our interest to accentuate, and our thoughts to be stimulated.

> We can concentrate on the details of a strong source of inspiration.

If we 'act' on an inspirational source, we are likely to connect with it and remember it for longer.

Tangible sources of inspiration retain a physical presence.

Intangible sources of inspiration provide a physical experience that can be retained to some extent as a memory, and in some instances they can also be reignited.

We can strengthen intangible sources of inspiration by recording the details and qualities of our experiences.

Inspiration is important for creativity because it can illuminate our thoughts and give us a stimulus for new ideas.

Artists, inventors, and scientists all need inspiration to progress their ideas.

When we create something non-physical, such as a formula, our minds have to comprehend the creation.

Curiosity can help us to find inspiration for creativity.

Key Points

Looking 'beyond what exists' can help us to develop 'what doesn't exist'.

Inspiration can arrive without looking, but we still need to be receptive to inspiration if we are to register it in our minds.

Finding the qualities in a person who inspires us can provide us with a resource to inspire our own lives.

Identifying the avenues we can take with inspiration can help us to be creative, as well as help us to see much more than the subject of our inspiration.

A List of Inspirational People can become a resource of the people who have inspired us and the qualities we admire and value.

An Inspirational Sourcebook can become a resource for inspiring our minds.

When we apply our inspiration, we have eight identifiable choices.

Interpreting the way we apply our inspiration takes us to a much more detailed level.

Interpreting our inspiration allows us to show our individuality and our ideas, and it also allows us to explore our minds.

Key Points

A Radial Approach for Applying Inspiration is the way we can use one or more sources of inspiration to aid creativity.

A Linear Record of Inspiration is a way of identifying the links between one inspirational source and another.

CHAPTER 4   IMAGINATION ACCESSORY

Creating mental images, sensations, and emotions that are not physically present at the time of creating and/or thinking in a creative and original way

Our imagination is a wonderful thing, not only because it enables us to *see* with our minds, but also because it can help us to experience sensations and emotions that are not physically present. Another important aspect of our imagination is that it allows us to think in a very unique and original way.

We can discover our imagination among the pages of numerous novels; they can provide us with the opportunity to convert descriptive details into images we can see, emotions we can feel, and senses we can relate to. Pictures of characters and scenes enter the screen of our mind's eye as we subconsciously glue them together and create our own visual, sensual, and emotional dialogue. We can really feel a sense of escape as our imagination transports our minds into another world, away from our reality and routine. We can journey to Far East Africa and experience a safari, watching elephants and giraffes roaming free, feeling the bumps on a red dust road as we travel in a four wheel drive, and desiring a bed at the end of the day as the exhaustion of heat and intrigue squeezes out our last drops of energy. Alternatively, we might enter the Edwardian era and experience the working day of servants in a large manor house….as the servants prepare for an evening banquet they are found to be polishing, cleaning, ironing, and cooking….all silver must shine, all fireplaces must burn, and all food must be spectacularly presented. The waiters regimentally lay out the dinner table, measuring the distances of every single piece of cutlery, china, silver, and glass, so that every single piece has its own designated place on the table.

Many of the scenes we envisage in our imagination are broadened from the initial descriptions we are given. It only takes a few words for us to conjure up pictures in our minds, as the descriptions of the above safari and Edwardian era clearly show. Our imagination brings in many of our *own* images as we attempt to envisage the descriptions being provided, and as we retrieve the pictures from our memory, we piece them together in such a way as to resemble the pictures that are being described.

Of course, we're probably much more aware of using our imagination for seeing images in our minds than we are of experiencing senses and emotions. But if we just think about some of our dreams, then we can begin to understand that not only do we see images in our imagination, but we can also experience our senses and emotions. Actors are a very good example of those who 'draw' from their imagination. They do this so they can express emotions such as sadness, or imagine senses such as the smell of a scented rose. Essentially, we draw images, senses, and emotions from our memory, and then we use them in our imagination to create our own original screenplay.

In our reality world, we use our imagination on a regular basis, but again we don't usually give it a second thought. Going house hunting is a typical example of where imagination can enter. We often need to use our imagination to look beyond the decor of a house and to visualise what it might become if we were to change the interior.

So how can we find our imagination? How can we use it? And what benefits can we gain? This is where our Imagination Accessory begins.

What Will I Learn?

You will learn about the way your visual memory can assist with much of what you see in your imagination, and how your memory of senses and emotions can also play a role. You will learn about the two visualisation processes that can enable you to see either your reality, or images that are entirely imaginary. And through these forms of visualisation, you will learn how to strengthen your imagination, and how to apply your Accessory in many different ways, such as for motivating, memorising, and rehearsing.

The theme of visualisation continues as you learn about the different ways of seeing with your mind's eye, and how you can control the speed of the images that pass across your mind. Moving on to your other senses of taste, touch, smell, and sound, you will be given the opportunity to recall memories of these senses and to experience them in your imagination. You will also have the opportunity to 'draw' on your feelings, and to imagine particular emotions that are related to certain experiences in your life.

You will learn about the links between creativity and imagination, including the different ways you can practise with creative images before you physically produce them. You will discover more about your sleeping and waking dreams, and the links with imagination. And you will be given the opportunity to think about the different ways you might 'connect' with your dreams. As you move on through the pages, you will be reminded of the assumptions that can be made when conjuring up pictures in your mind, and how this knowledge can be turned around to advance your imaginative thinking. And you will learn how to adapt your thinking by using your imagination, and how you can create the potential for new thoughts and ideas.

ASPECTS OF MEMORY
Visual Memory

Before we delve more deeply into the mysteries of our imagination, it is essential that we first understand where many of our images are coming from. While we might vaguely think that our imagination gives us pictures we've never seen before, many of those pictures don't actually come out of thin air; our imagination doesn't exist in a vacuum. Instead, much of what we see in our imagination comes first from the images we see in reality. Our visual memory stores many of these images, and our imagination uses them to form new mental pictures.

Our **visual memory** is the most predominant area that we call upon when we use our imagination. It's one of the most important and remarkable qualities of our minds, helping us to 'record and recall' images, such as childhood memories, the places we've lived, the people we've known, the paintings we've loved, the things we've done….. Our visual memory is a **resource for our minds**, containing knowledge, experiences, and other images that have passed across our eyes and become implanted in our minds.

Many of the images which become fixed in our visual memory are images we don't even think we've observed; we aren't aware of having studied them at any conscious level of detail. This is because many of the images in our visual memory have been recorded through our subconscious observation. If we see the same images repeatedly, then these images will become stronger in our minds, even though we may not be consciously observing them. Equally, if certain images hold some personal significance, then our subconscious will again record them as stronger images in our minds.

If we attempt to recall some of our **subconscious images**, they won't all be clear in our minds, and much of this has to do with the repetition and significance issues. Take an example of a train station, bus terminus, or airport that you've visited several times. You won't have consciously studied *every single aspect* of that place, and yet your visual memory can recall an amazing amount of detail if you try to remember the images. When we call up images from our visual memory, we can begin to appreciate the amazing way in which our minds see images, and the way we can use those images.

In recognising the way we can call images into our mind's eye, we can consider one of the most common uses of our visual memory, this being the way we can **plan things in our minds**. Most of the time we are totally unaware of the images that pop into our minds, such as thinking about a job we have to do, a place we have to be, a person we have to meet….. We become so accustomed to seeing these images in our minds that we become oblivious to their presence. As an illustration, you could think about the jobs you have to do in your home, maybe it's the washing, the ironing, or maybe you want to tidy a particular room.

Now think about the images that flashed across your mind as you thought about those jobs, they might have only been there for a millisecond in time, but they were there nonetheless. So even in the simplest of ways, our ability to call upon our visual memory enables us to plan things in our minds.

We can now take a small step forwards to think about the way our visual memory becomes our own **Visual Encyclopaedia**. We already know that we don't bring a conscious awareness to everything we see in our lives, but somehow, our visual memory is able to absorb what we see, and also to '**label**' those images so that we can recall them more easily. These labels are consciously and subconsciously placed on our images, and can include our written and spoken language, our emotions, and our senses. The most common labels we use come first from our language, so we can recall the images of a pencil, desk, or chair because we've labelled those images with the words that represent them. When it comes to our emotions, we can recall images of when we were happy, as well as when we were sad, and we can do this by referring to the emotional labels we've placed on specific images. We also use our senses in this way, so we might label the image of a roast dinner with the smell of steaming gravy, or the image of a French café with the smell of ground coffee. So our language, emotions, and senses can provide our images with a '**location**' in our Visual Encyclopaedia, and enable us to recall specific images in our minds.

Memory of Senses and Emotions

We've already learned about the memory of one of our senses, being our visual memory, so in this section I want to briefly discuss the memory of our other senses, of taste, touch, smell, and sound (TTSS), and also our memory of emotions.

It's worth acknowledging at this point that our minds have **memories of our TTSS senses and emotions** as distinctive from our visual memory, but because much of what we sense and feel becomes so entwined with our visual memory, our TTSS senses and emotions can become **inextricably linked** to our Visual Encyclopaedia. This again is the reason why we're able to call up certain images in our minds simply by thinking about a particular taste, touch, smell, sound, or emotion.

Our memory of TTSS senses enables us to recall information, such as the taste of a banana, the touch of leather, the smell of exhaust fumes, or the sound of a favourite song. It's only when we begin to *really* think about our memory of TTSS senses that we can begin to realise the enormous amount of information we record.

Give yourself a few moments and recall some of the sensations below:

> Sourness of bitter lemon
> Sweetness of sugar
> Smoothness of velvet

> Temperature of hot water
> Aroma of baking bread
> Fumes from a bonfire
> Beauty of a bird song
> Noise of a lawn mower

While our recollection of TTSS senses might *feel* more vague than our recollection of visual memories, they are there nonetheless, and if we concentrate on them, we have the potential to make them stronger in our minds.

* * * * * *

Now we come to our memory of emotions. There's a vast array of emotions out there in the world, and we collect them as we travel throughout our lives. Having added these emotions to our memory, we then have the capacity to recall them, and we can do this more easily by recalling specific experiences that initiated those emotions. So if we think of a situation when we were sad, not only can we visualise that situation, but we can also recapture the emotion of being sad – we can remember what it feels like to be sad.

Give yourself a few moments and have a look at the examples below:

> An occasion when I felt happy

> A situation when I felt frustrated

A time when I felt elated

A moment when I was contented

So our memory can actually help us to recall situations where we've experienced certain emotions. Our minds Encyclopaedia, then, becomes a resource for our life experiences, including our senses of sight, taste, touch, smell, and sound, and the emotions we've experienced throughout our lives.

Memory of Non-Reality Images & Senses

We've learned that many of the images in our visual memory are those that we collect from the *reality* we see, but there is yet another dimension to this area of our memory, and that is, the **non-reality images we collect from our imagination**. We retain a vast array of non-reality images from our imagination, including many from our sleeping dreams and daydreams. We may also recall some of the experimental ideas we've conjured up in our minds, such as attempting to create something new. So our visual memory is constantly expanding through our constant view of reality and through our memory of the non-reality images we've created in our imagination. It's a Visual Encyclopaedia that keeps growing, changing, and evolving over time, and it's an invaluable resource for our minds.

But wait a minute…there's more. Where our TTSS senses are concerned, we don't seem to be able to 'create' new sensations for taste, touch, and smell in our imagination, but we do seem to be able to **create new sounds**, such as a song in our minds, or words we haven't spoken before. In our sleeping dreams, we can certainly *recall* our senses of sight, taste, touch, smell, and sound, and adapt them to the new situations we dream about, but it's only our senses of sight and sound in our imagination that allow us to create entirely new non-reality situations. The new sounds we create can be from thoughts we have in the day, or dreams we have at night, and both can become linked to our vast minds Encyclopaedia.

Curiosity

Curiosity has a key role to play in the development of our imagination. As human beings we're naturally very curious....we inspect things, we want to know more, we want to understand how things work, to learn why something is the way it is....we want to know who, when, where, and why....we want to learn..... We aren't curious all the time, partly because this would be enormously time consuming, but also because we aren't always interested in being curious. The main point I'm making here is that we gain information from being curious, and some of this information becomes lodged in our memory. We then have the potential to use what we record from our curiosity and apply it with our imagination, both consciously and subconsciously.

If we subdue our curiosity and let life pass us by, then our imagination will also be affected. Instead, if we choose to be more curious about the world around us and delve more deeply into the experience of living, then we can record these details in our memory, and create the potential to reignite our imagination.

VISUAL MEMORY

When we create our **imaginative images**, the first thing we do (mostly without realising it) is select images from our Visual Encyclopaedia. The images we select might be those we've seen in our reality or those we've previously created in our imagination. Then, once we've selected our images, we 'adapt' them in our imagination and create the image which is being described (either by ourselves or by someone else).

Adapting our images from reality is the key to understanding how we create many of the images we see in our imagination; we select an image we know, and then adapt it in some way. For example, we can picture a white soccer ball in our imagination…and then adapt the image to a pink soccer ball, or we can picture a chair with four legs in our imagination…and then adapt it to a chair with five legs. So when we use our Visual Memory with Imagination, we take the 'framework' of an image we have in our Visual Encyclopaedia and change it in the way we describe.

If we adapt our pictures quickly, then we probably

won't even begin to think where our original pictures are coming from (i.e. whether they're coming from images we've seen in our reality or from images we've previously 'made up' in our imagination). If we adapt our images more slowly and precisely, then we might be more aware of where our pictures have originated. *"And why is it important to know where our pictures are coming from?"* I hear you say. Well, it's all about recognising and strengthening our Imagination Accessory. If we become more aware of the images we're recalling from reality, then we can attempt to see them more clearly in our minds and try to concentrate on more of the **details**. If we become more aware of the images we've previously 'made up' in our imagination, then again we can try to see the images more clearly in our minds, and we can additionally recognise their value as entirely 'original' images.

We can experience the sensation of calling up images in our minds and then adapting them in our imagination by taking ourselves through the description below. By making ourselves more conscious of the images we see and the adaptations we introduce, we can learn to *access* our imagination more easily. If we experiment further by adding our emotions and TTSS senses, then we can make our images even stronger in our minds and strengthen our ability to handle three complex aspects at once – of seeing our images, feeling our emotions, and imagining our four other senses (of taste, touch, smell and sound). Our emotions and TTSS senses help to enrich what we see in our imagination and can make our images more meaningful.

As you make your way through the description below (*and try to go through it slowly so that you can really see the images in your mind*), concentrate on the details of the images described and also encourage your senses and emotions to become part of the scene:

> Consider the image of a Christmas tree in the front lounge of your house. At first you notice some of the details in your lounge, such as the sofa, carpet, and lights. Then you focus on the Christmas tree with its decorations of gold and red tinsel, brightly coloured baubles (with some in the shape of bells), Christmas tree lights, and a huge yellow ribbon tied around the middle.
>
> As you move up to the tree, you can smell the pine aroma, and when you touch the tree, you can feel the sharpness of its pine needles. You run your hands along the tinsel and feel the cold smooth texture against your palms. You shake one of the bells and hear it ring against its metal surround. You look at the presents that have been wrapped and placed at the bottom of the tree. You notice all the different types of wrapping paper, some with pictures, and others of a glistening gold or silver.

The images you created in your picture would have commenced with images you've seen in your reality (and recorded in your visual memory). You then adapted those images in order to wrap them around the descriptions provided. Because the Christmas tree was in the front lounge of your house, you had the potential to add a substantial amount of detail to your picture, as you quickly imagined some of the key features of your lounge. You were then presented with different objects as an adaptation of objects that you've probably seen in reality. The introduction of sensations would have intensified the scene and assisted you in forming the images in your mind. And by combining the images and sensations, you may well have conjured up some emotions, such as excitement or anticipation; the type of emotions you might have had as a child on Christmas day. The **more we describe an image,** not only through the visual content but also using our other four senses, the **clearer it will become in our minds** and the more likely our emotions will additionally be aroused.

If we try to call up an image that isn't in our visual memory, then we can certainly try to create an image in our minds, but it might not be the *correct* image. For example, if I asked you to imagine a 'trooler', then it would be difficult for you to see this in your mind because you don't know what a 'trooler' is. If I then told you it was a type of food, then you might conjure up something in your mind, but again, without additional description or without actually seeing it for yourself, it would be difficult for you to retrieve a correct picture in your mind or even any picture at all. If we're unaware of what a particular description refers to, it becomes more difficult for us to see it in our imagination, and we can often struggle to come up with anything at all. If we're given sufficient detail to create a picture in our imagination, then we can visualise it more easily.

Authentic and Adapted Visualisation

So far, we've learned the way our imagination can help us to **visualise reality images** and **visualise non-reality images**. Our Visual Encyclopaedia provides us with the framework for using both types of visualisation, because we can call up authentic images and either visualise them authentically, or adapt them in some way. Essentially, then, we can identify these two different forms of visualisation as 'Authentic Visualisation' and 'Adapted Visualisation'.

Authentic Visualisation allows us to call up a childhood memory, a favourite meal, a first job, a favourite TV show, pictures from a magazine…..etc. We can visualise an event we recently attended, such as a birthday party, wedding, or an evening out, and recall various moments of that event as we visualise them authentically in our minds. We can recall the roads we regularly take to work and visualise the features of our journey, so that we can describe them to ourselves or to someone else. Of course, our

Authentic Visualisation might not be 100% accurate because we might forget some of the details, or unconsciously embellish them a little. Nevertheless, the essential criteria for classifying the way we visualise as 'authentic' is that we are attempting to recall a visual memory of something from our reality.

Adapted Visualisation allows us to change the images we've recorded from our reality. For example, we can call up an image of a rubbish bin – it might be a round bin, a black bin, a green 'wheelie' bin, or some other type of bin – and then we can take that image and put two car wheels on the bottom of the rubbish bin. We've changed our image by using the process of Adapted Visualisation. We've enabled our minds to come up with a 'new view' of the images that we've recorded from reality. When we use Adapted Visualisation, our images might become completely obscure from our reality, such as a giant with two eyes and three arms, or they might relate more closely to our reality, such as the scene of the Christmas tree previously described.

The following list provides some examples of the different ways we might use Authentic and Adapted visualisation. The list is not exhaustive but it provides some of the more common situations where the two different forms of visualisation might apply:

Authentic Visualisation (recalling images from our reality)

Recalling authentic images from our Visual Encyclopaedia – such as our house, our furniture, a baseball hat, an electric frying pan, a hairbrush, a coat hanger. We can recall the images that are known to us.

Recalling the meaning of icons we've learned – such as the icons on a computer or on our mobile phone. Our Visual Encyclopaedia helps us to recognise these images so that we can instinctively select the action we want.

Thinking about and planning the jobs we need to do – such as doing the washing, cleaning the car, and getting food out of the freezer.

Calling up a personal memory – such as people, places, and experiences from our reality.

Conversing with others about our reality – such as describing a movie we watched, a meal we cooked, or the clothes we bought in a sale.

Unwinding from our day – re-visualising what occurred in our day and unwinding with our thoughts.

Adapted Visualisation (recalling images from our reality and adapting them)

Daydreaming – such as imagining what a friend might be doing, dreaming of a place we would rather be, or visualising people from a favourite drama.

Sleepy dreaming (when we're not quite awake, and not quite asleep) – just before we drop off to sleep, or when we've started to wake up, we can sometimes see images in our imagination. We might even have some control over these images and attempt to create our own storyline.

Dreaming when asleep – when we remember our dreams, we can come across a whole array of images. Our dreams can include humour, emotion, inventions, people we know, people we don't know, and also our senses of taste, touch, smell, and sound. Sometimes we can have the same dream several times.

Visualising our goals and motivating our minds – seeing ourselves in a situation we know, and adding some adapted images that will motivate us, such as visualising ourselves winning a prize, or visualising where we want to be in two years' time.

Being creative and imaginative – such as thinking about the design of a garden, the creation of a painting, or the progression of an idea. This also includes practising and making mistakes in our minds before we physically produce something.

Memorising through visualisation – using strange and funny images to help us to recall things more easily, such as a swan jumping onto a ball and balancing a walking stick on its head (these images representing the numbers 2 0 1).

Rehearsing a scene – this can be similar to motivating ourselves, but it's slightly different. Its main purpose is to prepare ourselves. We might visualise ourselves apologising to someone and anticipating their reactions.

Seeing in our Minds

Before we continue to discover more about our imagination, let's take a brief look at that amazing 'screen' we see in our minds every time we visualise. Seeing with our imagination is like watching our own television screen, with **our mind's eye** as the screen and our brain as the selector of channels. We can flash up images on our mental screen and select what we want to see, or we can allow images to appear freely in our minds. And as we see our images, we can take our minds through an amazing array of pictures and thoughts.

It's probably even easier for us to comprehend if we imagine ourselves projecting images onto our own

movie screen and feel ourselves consciously attempting to control our projection. For example, we can project on our screen a man dressed in a black suit, a yellow bowler hat, and a bright pink tie. We can tell him to walk towards a big yellow bird and shake hands with that bird (or shake a hand and a wing!). We can focus on a newspaper that the man is carrying under his arm, and get him to open up that newspaper and look at the front page. We can see a picture on the front page that shows a man in a black suit and a yellow bowler hat shaking hands with a big yellow bird. So, consciously projecting images on our mental screen is one way of trying to understand our imagination and to enhance our incredible ability of seeing in our minds.

There is yet another way in which we can consider 'seeing with our minds', and that is to view our mental screen like an **artist's canvas**. When we use our mind's eye like an artist's canvas, we can consciously attempt to build up a range of different layers (like layers of paint on a canvas) and then try to visualise those layers individually, as well as visualise the whole picture. In other words, as we gradually build up a picture in our minds, we can choose to view each of our images as separate transparent overlays, containing only a partial component of an overall picture. We can then place those overlays onto our canvas, and continue to add or remove them as we dictate. Viewing this building up of layers can help us to have more control over what we visualise, and we can learn to move various images around on our canvas. Building with layers is often a subconscious process, but in becoming more aware of this process, we can choose to use it consciously, and decide when we want to apply it.

Below is an example of using 'the artist's canvas' to visualise in our minds. As you read through the example, try to develop the layers in your mind, and notice how you're able to control what you see:

> Imagine a desert scene with a very high sand dune, two camels at the top of the sand dune, and each camel carrying one person.
>
> In the foreground, you see a red telephone box.
>
> Looking up, you see a beautiful topaz sky.

Try to visualise this picture in your mind's eye before you read on.

> Now that you've created your picture, take away the layer of the red telephone box, and replace it with a blue mailbox.
>
> Next, change your assumed sand colour of beige, to the colour orange.
>
> Finally, change the blue sky to white.

Make sure you can still visualise the two camels, and the people riding on them.

If you registered the picture in your mind as layers, you should have been able to adjust those layers one at a time, and re-adjust the picture in your mind. It's certainly not the easiest thing to do, and it becomes more complicated as the number of layers increase, however, you can really make your mind work with this type of exercise, and by practising with your artist's canvas you can strengthen this valuable ability of your mind.

As I mentioned above, seeing with our minds through the process of the artist's canvas is a very useful way to create pictures in our minds, and also to *control* those pictures. Images that are created through the artist's canvas can more easily be adapted in our minds than images without any recognisable layers. Of course, if we continually make changes to the layers of our picture, or add excessive amounts of detail, then it can become more difficult for us to 'hold' each new image in our minds. By practising with the artist's canvas, we can enhance our memory (since we're learning to carry a range of pictures and keeping them in the background of our minds) and come up with creative ideas that we might never have thought of (since layering can provide us with some interesting and sometimes obscure results).

Speed and Clarity

Images enter the screen of our mind's eye every day of our lives. Many of them appear within **milliseconds** of each other and pass freely in the background of our minds. Many others stay longer in our minds, particularly if they are of interest to us, evoke certain feelings, or relate to something we're anxious about. Of course, it would be impossible for us to consciously acknowledge *all* of the images that pass through our minds every day because they are **innumerable in quantity.** We know we don't 'tune in' to every image in our minds, because it would consume too much of our time and mental energy, and also limit our ability to carry out other mental activities. Instead, we're vaguely aware of some of the images we see (such as seeing our laundry when we plan to do some washing), and other images can become gradually stronger in our minds, depending on their relative importance or familiarity. The point to note here is that if we become more aware of the images that pass across our minds, then we can start to consciously control some of those images, and slow them down, and even see them in more detail. We can *exercise* our ability to imagine.

If we choose to slow down selected images in our minds, then we have to look at them in more detail in order to discern them more clearly, and in attempting to see our images more clearly, we can end up adding our own **detail and definition**. If we concentrate on the details that we build up in our images, then we can begin to bring our images into **clearer focus** and create a stronger memory of those images. Having created this stronger memory, we can then recall those images more easily and we can choose to perceive them for longer. By understanding and utilising our ability to consciously control our images, we can directly affect their speed and clarity, and increase our ability to visualise and memorise images. Indirectly, our capacity to use our imagination will expand, because we're adding new and defined details to our Visual Encyclopaedia. So the speed and clarity of selected images can become a conscious decision for our minds, and we can expand and explore a further dimension of our mental abilities.

SENSUAL & EMOTIONAL MEMORY

In the previous section 'Memory of senses and emotions', we learned that we have a memory of our four senses of taste, touch, smell, and sound, and also a memory of our emotions. We learned that such memories can become inextricably linked to our Visual Encyclopaedia, partly because our sense of sight is usually our most dominant sense. In this section I want to explore in more detail the link between our imagination and our recollection of senses and emotions.

To help us to understand the way our memory of senses and emotions can be used in our imagination, we can use the symbolism of our memories being rather like digital cards on a computer. So we can think of our individual memories as being recorded on a range of **Memory Cards**. On each of our Memory Cards we record our experiences. So for each of our five senses we have an individual Memory Card, and for each of our emotions we have a Memory Card. By using this symbolism, we can now begin to explore the use of our sensual and emotional memory with our imagination.

Imagining TTSS Senses

Our Memory Cards for our four senses of taste, touch, smell, and sound (TTSS) contain a vast array of the senses which we've experienced in our lives, and they grow continually as we move throughout our lives. We can tend to forget our TTSS senses because we become so accustomed to them, and because we don't always allow ourselves to focus on them as strongly as our sense of sight. Nevertheless, our minds record a significant amount of detail for these senses, and we often do this subconsciously.

One way in which we use our **TTSS Memory Cards** is when we want to assess something we're experiencing in the present, against our memory of a past experience. For example, if we smell a mango for the first time, we might relate the smell to a pineapple and an apricot if we already have those smells on our Memory Card. The point to make here is that we can 'call up' a memory of the senses we've experienced, and we can bring them into our imagination as we choose (although it can feel more difficult for us to do this for our TTSS Memory Cards than for our Visual Memory Card).

Just as you've learned about Authentic Visualisation and Adaptive Visualisation, our TTSS senses can also be viewed in this way. Imagine, for example, the touch of a white feather – you can feel the softness and delicate nature of the feather, and you can feel some of the many strands that make up the feather. Now, imagine you're running your fingers gently down a rough rendered wall – you can feel a few sharp bits here and there, and the roughness of the ups and downs of the rendering. Both of the latter descriptions should help you to imagine your sense of touch, as well as your sense of sight (that is, you should be able to imagine what's being described with the aid of your memory of touch and sight). To enhance the fact that you're using your imagination, try now to place the white feather over the surface of the rendered wall, and then feel both of them together – you might still feel the softness of the feather, but you should also feel the ups and downs of the rough rendering underneath the feather.

In the above example, you imagined authentically the white feather and the rough rendered wall, and then adapted those images as you placed the feather over the rough rendered wall. In both situations, you're imagining the sensations, but you use your *memory* of sight and touch to assist you with your imagined scene.

Some more examples to recall and imagine are given below. Try to imagine them as authentically as you can, and give yourself a few moments to imagine each of them:

> The taste of an orange
>
> The touch of silk
>
> The smell of garlic
>
> The sound of a ticking clock

Now, with the taste of a piece of orange in your mouth, take a silk scarf and wrap it around a whole orange, and tie it at the top. Next, crush a few cloves of strong smelling garlic, and become aware of a loud ticking clock.

In the above example, you have again experienced your senses authentically and then adaptively.

Imagining Emotions

So now we come to the labyrinth of our **Emotional Memory Cards** and the way they interact with our imagination. Where to start. Well, we know that our emotions cover an enormous range. We know that we can recall certain emotional experiences. And we know that we can be at the mercy of our emotions, or we can learn to take control over the way we feel. So where does this take us with imagining our emotions?

> It takes us to the beginning.........and it takes us to the beginning.

I know that sounds rather odd, but what I mean by the above is that if we begin to recollect certain emotions in our minds, and bring them into our imagination, then we can start to experience and understand their qualities more deeply. We can also strengthen our ability to 'call them up' in our minds. If we continually bring new emotions into our minds, and understand them more deeply in our imagination, then we might begin to see that even one emotion has many different layers inside it. So happiness, for example, can cover a whole spectrum of different emotions and can be found in a whole spectrum of different situations. In fact, we have so many emotions we aren't even aware of because we tend to define them too broadly. So while we're at the beginning of recalling emotions in our imagination, we can then find ourselves at the beginning again, because we can keep on discovering more and more layers within each of our emotions. And as we continually experience our emotions throughout our lives, we have the capacity to add these to our ever growing labyrinth of emotional memories.

Another interesting aspect of our emotional memory and imagination is that we have the potential to actually convince ourselves that we feel a certain way. Take a look at the following example:

> I can remember the feeling of being happy..... I also felt engrossed and contented..... I can imagine the feeling of being happy..... I can prolong my imagined feeling in my mind by concentrating on the word 'happy'..... I can bring in other feelings in my mind that are associated with being happy..... I am starting to actually *feel* happy..... Now I *do* feel happy.

Of course, the above result doesn't happen immediately. It would take time and meditation with each of the above sentences to really begin to feel happy in our minds. But what the above example attempts to illustrate is that we can authentically bring an emotion into our imagination, and gradually adapt our thoughts so that we can begin to really *feel* our emotion in our minds.

Some people who meditate with emotions can help themselves feel a certain way simply by concentrating on that particular emotion, and through their practice and repetition, they can develop a degree of control over the emotions they feel. So they might choose to be calm in a time of crisis, or choose to feel happy despite the negative vibes that are being sent out by other people. This doesn't mean they aren't compassionate or caring people, it means that they can use their emotional memory with imagination in a positive way, to help themselves – and often indirectly to help others around them.

So our Emotional Memory Cards are numerous, and we store a whole range of experiences on each of them. If we become more consciously aware of the individual emotions we feel, then we can define our Emotional Memory Cards more readily, and have the capacity to call up a range of different feelings when we bring them into our imagination. Actors use their Emotional Memory Cards substantially. They learn to bring specific emotions into their minds and try to capture them in the essence of a character or a particular scene.

By remembering what certain emotions feel like, we might even try to experience more of the emotions we like, and less of those we don't like. Of course, external and unforeseen events can always impinge on our positive emotions, but by using our memory, we can try to take ourselves back to our positive emotions and move away from the negative side. We still retain a memory of the more negative emotions because this gives us a 'measure' of our emotional spectrum, but we can choose to concentrate on our positive emotions.

And of course, let's not forget that when we recall a situation where we experienced a certain emotion, we're attempting to imagine our emotion 'authentically'. When we call up that feeling and consciously apply it to a situation, such as acting out a scene in a play, we use that emotion adaptively. Our emotions, then, can be imagined authentically or adaptively.

THE DIVERSITY OF IMAGINATION

We know that our imagination is diverse. We can use it consciously in our day, or subconsciously through our sleeping dreams, daydreams, and sleepy dream states (occurring just before we go to sleep, and just before we wake up). We can also use our imagination when we read a novel, listen to music, or study the details of a painting. And we can actively use it as a tool for our minds; to be creative, to practice, to memorise, to motivate, to rehearse, and to relax. So the diversity of our imagination encompasses the way we can **use it consciously and subconsciously**, the range of **sources that can trigger our imagination**, and the different ways we can use our imagination as **a tool for our minds**.

Conscious and Subconscious

We've already learned that when we **observe** our images, we do so both consciously and subconsciously, and that numerous images end up in our visual memory. We also know that we observe consciously and subconsciously with our four senses of taste, touch, smell, and sound, and that these also become recorded as memories. And we've learned that we can use our visual memory, and to some extent our memory of senses and emotions, to select images and sensations and **adapt them** in our minds by using our imagination. Phew!

When we use our conscious imagination, we have the opportunity to add a range of details to our images and to play around with them in our minds. Creative people in particular use conscious imagination to come up with creative ideas and to 'think outside the square'. Becoming more aware of our conscious imagination can in its own right assist us in accessing our imagination more readily, and by consciously activating our imagination, we can make it a stronger Accessory in our minds.

Subconscious imagination occurs when we daydream and when we dream at night, and it can often provide us with some of our most interesting and unusual images. In developing and strengthening our Imagination Accessory, our subconscious imagination has an important role to play because we can see images that we might never have thought of at a conscious level. Maybe of even more importance, however, is the way we can strengthen a dimension of our memory by recalling images from our subconscious imagination. For example, do you remember your dreams? Do you consciously think about some of your daydreams? If we improve our memory of some of the images and other sensations we produce, then we can widen the ability of our minds to memorise, and we can continue to open up new possibilities.

Improving our memory of subconscious imagination starts by becoming more aware of it, and then by writing down what we can remember as soon as we become consciously responsive again. That means writing down the memory of a sleeping dream as soon as we come back to reality, or at the very least, writing down a few key words of our dreams so that we can recall them later. Those few key words can serve as trigger words to remind us about the content of our dreams, and with practice we have the potential to remember more and more of the detail of our dreams. Even daydreams can be interesting to record, and sometimes we can learn from them if we try to analyse them.

Dreaming

When we dream, the **free reign of our subconscious** selects images, emotions, senses, and thoughts and reconstructs them into something new. We can dream about a place; maybe somewhere we've visited or somewhere we want to visit. We can dream about people; maybe someone we know or someone we've created in a dream. We can find ourselves inventing **our own dialogue** in our dreams; we might be talking to a group of people or listening to other people. It's quite common to dream about conversing with others about something we've recently understood or committed to memory. It's information or knowledge which is fresh in our minds and which our subconscious has become very aware of. And, of course, we can dream with our senses, such as hearing music in our dreams, listening to ourselves singing, or feeling a piece of fabric.

When we recall our dreams, we might be able to trace them to some thoughts we had that evening, or to memories of some time ago, or to a television programme we watched that night. If we're worried about something, then we can often discover those worries in our dreams, but most likely in a slightly disguised format, so that we can only trace our dream details by re-assessing our worries. We can also have many dreams that don't seem to relate to anything we can think of; we can't imagine where they've come from. Our subconscious can jumble up our thoughts and images to such a degree that we can end up with a very confused dream, and a very odd storyline (and sometimes a very entertaining one as well!).

Essentially, we can experience anything in our dreams that we are aware of in our reality. And the more we become aware of our emotions and senses in reality, the more likely we are to experience them in our dreams, making them feel more alive and vibrant. This is one of the reasons why some of our dreams can feel so real, because they can incorporate many of our authentic images, emotions, and senses. Occasionally, we might get one of those dreams that is *so* authentic and vivid that when we wake up, we wonder whether our memory is of a dream or a memory of reality. We might even have to check with someone the next day to find out if a particular situation really happened or not.

Three Ways of Connecting with Sleeping Dreams

One of the most interesting aspects of our dreams is to become aware of the three different ways we can **connect** with our dreams. One of the ways we can connect is as the **viewer**; we watch our dream unfold as we sleep, but we don't actually see an image of ourselves in our dream, or anything else that might represent who we are in reality. We connect with our dream as the viewer, and maybe also through the emotions and senses we might experience in our dream.

I can remember having a dream where I was the viewer. It was an animated dream, which made it even more unusual. The key character in my dream was a small knitted yellow duck with piercing black eyes (a duck that actually exists in reality, believe it or not). It was like watching a feature length comedy because I could recall myself laughing at certain points in the dream. In one of the scenes, two boats were out at sea on a fishing trip. One boat was captained by the yellow duck, and the other by a fluffy white bear. They had the idea that if they draped a fishing net between the two boats (so that it looked like a type of catamaran) they could trawl the waters together and collect more fish. The idea seemed to work until a storm arose, by which time both boats were getting battered about. Somehow, the duck managed to save the white bear and they made it back to dry land in one piece. The next scene showed the fluffy white bear lying down on a wooden bench, coughing and spluttering up water. The bear managed to raise his head slightly and looking at the duck he said "Kiss me Hardy", and an audience laughed somewhere in the background of my mind. What a strange dream – I'm sure my wildest imagination would never have been able to come up with something so strange and funny.

Another way we can connect with our dreams is if we **appear as ourselves**. When we're present in our dreams, we can be aware of our movements as well as our emotions and senses, and we can physically interact with our surroundings and the people around us. I remember quite a strange dream I had one night, some of which made sense, while the rest was quite obscure. There were two baby elephants in the dream, a man in a wheel chair, and myself. The man in the wheelchair had an intense desire to walk again, and for some reason I could feel this intense desire inside of me. Strangely, I felt there was some sort of bond between us, so that his intense desire to walk again was also my intense desire for him. He sat in his wheel chair between the two elephants while I watched him from several feet away. Then I remember saying quite distinctly to him *"emotions can be **very** strong in our lives – they can push us forwards"*. I know I said this as I wrote it down immediately I woke up from my dream. After I said those words, I saw the man get up from his wheel chair, and with very slow and strained steps, he started to walk towards me. I could feel there was a strong emotional connection between us as he made those strenuous steps and I could see how he was using our emotional connection to achieve something that was seemingly impossible. I could feel the emotions he was feeling, and the energy he was feeling. I had a strong sense he just wanted to reach out to me, and we were both channelling our intense emotions so he could walk towards me. I seemed to be frozen from where I was standing, so I couldn't reach out to physically help him. It was only through our strong emotional connection that he was able to walk towards me.

The above dream really identifies the way our emotions can be strongly present in our dreams. Emotions are powerful in our reality world, but they can also be very powerful in our dreams. The above dream also shows that while we can appear as ourselves in our dreams, we can also take on other people's feelings, and understand some of the characters we create. We can end up with a whole range of complex characters and situations, and this can become more evident if we attempt to analyse our dreams in detail.

Another way we can connect with our dreams is if we **appear as someone or something else**. We know that we're in the dream, but the form we take is different to the form we have in reality. So we might be a human being, but not the person we see in the mirror every morning. Connecting in this way can be for many different reasons, and I certainly don't have all the answers, but it seems to me that one of the key components that is common to these types of dream, is that we *relate* in some way to the person or thing we portray. It's like watching a movie and relating to the feelings of someone in that movie, we can become so absorbed that we 'become' that person; we can feel scared when they are in danger, or emotionally upset when they are sad. Dreaming in this way enables us to be someone or something else, to see another perspective if you like, maybe even to learn something from our dreams if we can recall them and analyse them. I had an example of this type of dream when I imagined I was someone from a different period of time. I was dressed in a period costume and looked entirely different to the physical form I have in reality, but my mind was definitely contained within that person, with all my thoughts, senses, and emotions.

Sleepy Dream States

So far we've concentrated on our sleeping dreams, but we also need to look at our 'sleepy' dream states, those times when we're not quite asleep and not quite awake. In these semi-conscious moments, our mental screen can flicker with all sorts of images, and it's at those times that we can **choose to take some control.** We have a certain level of awareness of our images, so we can actually begin to dictate what happens in our imagination. For example, we might try to continue the storyline of an enjoyable dream, or change the direction of a negative dream into something more positive. Of course, we can't gain control every time we're in a sleepy dream state, but there are times when the opportunity arises in our minds. It's then up to us if we want to experiment a little and take some control over what we sense and feel.

Sleepy dream states can also provide us with our most **imaginative and creative moments**. They are the times when a solution we've been searching for can suddenly pop into our heads. Part of this is probably to do with the relaxed nature of our minds as we prepare ourselves for rest and sleep, or alternatively when we awake from a recharged sleeping slumber. Unfortunately, we don't always make the most of these moments because we simply allow our thoughts to pass on by, but if we choose to write down our creative thoughts, either in full or as key trigger words (in the same way we can write down key trigger words from a dream), then we can 'off load' our thoughts as we prepare for sleep, or as we wake up, and then come back to our key words once our minds are active again. Being more aware of our semi-conscious thoughts is not intended to cause insomnia, instead, the purpose is to enable our imagination to flourish at a different level.

Novels

Now we come to some of the sources of our imagination, such as novels, music, and paintings. We know that one of the most useful sources for stimulating our imagination is reading a good novel. We can find ourselves visiting the past, the present, or the future; journeying to far off lands; becoming an explorer; seeing life through someone else's eyes…….. Novels allow us to go anywhere, be anyone, see anything, and even pass through the gateways of time. They bring our imagination alive and allow us to enter an **illusionary world**, diverting our minds from our everyday lives.

When we read the descriptions in a novel, we instinctively bring up images and thoughts in our minds as we re-create the scenes and characters. Sometimes the descriptions cause our emotions and senses to enter our imaginary scenes, and even more so if we relate to any of the descriptions through personal experience. In other words, while the author creates the framework for our images, emotions, and senses, we also bring in **our own life experiences into the equation**, providing additional depth to the visual, emotional, and sensual dialogue. Our imagination can go far beyond what is explicitly stated in a novel because we can end up creating our own images, adding our own details, and exploring some of the feelings which are generated in the novel. And as we grow and learn from our own life experiences, we might find ourselves picking up a book we've read in the past, and gain **new meanings and insights** as we discover more from the words disclosed.

With some of our favourite novels, we can end up holding the 'essence' of that story for months or even years to come (depending on its content or influence in our lives). We can remember the feelings it conveyed, even if we've long forgotten exact quotes or scenes. We can remember what we 'received' from a favourite novel; it might have been an emotional outlet, a trigger for re-thinking our directions, a journey we related to, or a basis for instilling new thoughts and values. The very best novels are much more than entertainment alone; they can help us to **learn about ourselves** as well as notice the world around us in a different way.

Exploring Novel Imagination

The following extract illustrates how we can easily conjure up images in our minds when we use our imagination. As you read through, become more aware of the images appearing in your mind, and in particular, the personal details you add to your images. Also, take note of any emotions and senses you become aware of, and the way they provide an increased depth to your images.

Extract from 'Jane Eyre' by Charlotte Bronte[5] (the scene is set in the early 1800s when Jane Eyre is just a child):

"Next day, by noon, I was up and dressed, and sat wrapped in a shawl by the nursery hearth. I felt physically weak and broken down: but my worst ailment was an unutterable wretchedness of mind: a wretchedness which kept drawing from me silent tears; no sooner had I wiped one salt drop from my cheek than another followed. Yet I thought, I ought to have been happy; for none of the Reeds were there; they were all gone out in the carriage with their mama; Abbot, too, was sewing in another room, and Bessie, as she moved hither and thither, putting away toys and arranging drawers, addressed to me every now and then a word of unwonted kindness. This state of things should have been to me a paradise of peace, accustomed as I was to a life of ceaseless reprimand and thankless fagging; but, in fact, my racked nerves were now in such a state that no calm could soothe, and no pleasure excite agreeably.

Bessie had been down into the kitchen, and she brought up with her a tart on a certain brightly painted china plate, whose bird of paradise, nestling in a wreath of convolvuli and rosebuds, had been wont to stir in me a most enthusiastic sense of admiration; and which plate I had often petitioned to be allowed to take in my hand in order to examine it more closely, but had always hitherto been deemed unworthy of such a privilege. This precious vessel was now placed on my knee, and I was cordially invited to eat the circles of delicate pastry upon it. Vain favour! Coming, like most other favours long deferred and often wished for, too late! I could not eat the tart: and the plumage of the bird, the tints of the flowers, seemed strangely faded: I put both plate and tart away. Bessie asked if I would have a book: the word *book* acted as a transient stimulus, and I begged her to fetch *Gulliver's Travels* from the library. This book I had again and again perused with delight; I considered it a narrative of facts, and discovered in it a vein of interest deeper than what I found in fairy tales: for as to the elves, having sought them in vain among foxglove leaves and bells, under mushrooms and beneath the ground-ivy mantling old wall-nooks, I had at length made up my mind to the sad truth that they were all gone out of England to some savage country where the woods were wider and thicker, and the population more scant, whereas, Lilliput and Brobdignag being, in my creed, solid parts of the earth's surface, I doubted not that I might one day, by taking a long voyage, see with my own eyes the little fields, houses, and trees, the diminutive people, the tiny cows, sheep, and birds of the one realm; and the corn-fields forest-high, the mighty mastiffs, the monster cats, the tower-like men and women, of the other. Yet, when this cherished volume was now placed in my hand – when I turned over its leaves, and sought in its marvellous pictures the charm I had, till now, never failed to find – all was eerie and dreary; the giants were gaunt goblins, the pigmies malevolent and fearful imps, Gulliver a most desolate wanderer in most dread and dangerous regions. I closed the book, which I dared no longer peruse, and put it on the table, beside the untested tart."

Music

Music has many different roles in our lives, and it can touch us in many different ways, so when it comes to using our 'imagination with music', this is only one of the many ways we can make a connection. We don't use our imagination with every piece of music we listen to, but when we do, we have the opportunity to interact and connect. We might think of a song we like and listen to it in our minds, or we might imagine *we* are the artist singing a song and visualise ourselves performing to a 'sell out' crowd. We might listen to a piece of music and allow it to carry our imagination to some far off place.

Connecting with music through our imagination varies from person to person because it depends on the style of music we listen to, whether it appeals to us or not, and whether we 'tune in' to our imagination.

Music is as vast as our different personalities; we have an infinite variety of musical styles to choose from. And performers can sit within a style, outside a style, become a hybrid of different styles, or create an entirely new style; music covers a vast arena. There are so many different styles of music that it would be difficult to say that all styles have the potential to connect with our imagination, but there are certainly a significant proportion that can.

So what about the 'appeal' of music? Not everyone likes the same piece of music. A piece of music that grates on our minds is certainly not going to assist us in making a connection with our imagination, but music we enjoy, inspires us, or opens our minds is definitely going to have a place in our imagination.

So what about the other point, of 'tuning in' to our imagination? This is where we need to think about our subconscious and conscious connection with music. Subconsciously, we can tune in to music with our imagination when, for example, we're working on a project and the music helps us to free up our minds so that our imaginative thinking can really start working. Somehow, music such as this can help us to 'get into the zone' of creating and can help us to move almost seamlessly through the solving of a problem, the progression of a project, or the development of an original idea (this is closely related, of course, to our Inspiration Accessory, and often results in our Accessories of Inspiration and Imagination being very difficult to separate in 'identity' terms).

Listening to cutting edge music can particularly trigger our imagination, because the unusual nature of what we hear can push our minds away from our normal thinking patterns, and allow us to enter areas of our minds where creative and original thinking can occur. It's also interesting to note that in some cases the 'beat' of musical rhythms can create a synergy with our minds, causing our thoughts to flow more easily, our creativity to feel more open, and our contentment levels to rise. In these situations, we can feel as if we're working 'alongside' our music, as the synergy of 'mind and rhythm' frees up our thoughts.

We can also tune in to 'music and imagination' at a conscious level, and think about where the music takes us, such as the scenes we create in our minds, the senses that are triggered, and the emotions we engage. Listening to classical music is an example of the way we can consciously connect with music and imagination. Claude Debussy's 'La mer' has the potential to take our imagination to many different places as we listen to the changing moods and expressions of the sea.[6] The first of the three symphonic sketches from La mer moves us from dawn to noon as we listen to the richness of the sea and its changing patterns. The second piece helps us to visualise the stirring of the wind and the sea as both begin to play and interact. The final piece is a much stronger conversation between wind and sea. The breeze becomes a storm, the storm becomes a wild beast, and the waves crash ceaselessly over each other and consume one wave after the other. Finally, we hear the full strength of the wind and sea as they unleash their combined power. Other classical pieces can also stir up our imagination. We can listen to musical representations of leaves rustling, thunder crashing, sirens singing, children playing, festivals stirring, and costumes swirling. These forms of musical representation can help us to open our imagination and discover our own interpretations; our minds can advance into another world.

Another example where music and imagination can work together is through the choreography of dance. Instead of using dance moves that are already known, a choreographer has the opportunity to create new moves and expressions, and to link these directly to music. Another example is in the composition of music and lyrics; in this creative field, imagination has a huge role to play.

Connect with music and imagination:
Become more aware of the types of music which trigger your imagination. Think about the images you form in your mind as you listen to particular pieces. Think about your senses and emotions, and consider whether various parts of the music trigger these qualities in your mind.

Creating

Creating in our minds is something we can **complement** with selected inspirational sources. With our Inspiration Accessory, we have eight identifiable choices when we want to apply our inspiration. But while these choices are important for creativity, we also need to use our imagination to achieve our creative ideas. Even if we choose to copy something that inspires us, we still need to use our imagination to think about how to create our copy. For example, if I want to copy a piece of engraved pottery, then I need to use my imagination to think about how to create the shape of the pottery and also how to achieve the etching.

Our imagination gives us a wonderful opportunity to **plan our creative ideas** before we physically produce them, and it can also assist us throughout the physical production stages. Many painters use their imagination to plan pictures and colours long before they put pastel to paper, or brush to canvas. Some even find themselves painting in their minds as a way of tackling problems before they encounter them physically. This process of 'creating in our minds' helps us not only to come up with images and ideas, but also to work through various methods of achieving what we want to produce.

Planning our creative ideas might involve adapting an image in our minds from something we've seen in a photograph, and imagining how to represent it in a material form. Alternatively, we might try to imagine something completely from scratch, something totally unique and original. As we work through our various thoughts, we can **practice with ideas in our minds** and potentially make the mistakes we might otherwise have made in a physical form. Making mistakes in our minds means that our **imagination can help us to learn**, because we can experiment with our thoughts and ideas, and gradually crystallise in our minds the physical form we want to produce. So it's possible for us to plan, practice, and learn through our imagination when we use it for creativity.

Of course, when we create in our minds, we use more than our imagination to create our thoughts and ideas; other areas of our minds, such as logic and analysis, also assist in the formulation of our thoughts. When we use logic for creativity, our brain tells us what is **appropriate or inappropriate**. For example, we can create a landscape in our minds of fields and trees, and see our image as a reflection of our reality, so we create a logical image. The colours of our logical landscape might be a light green for fields and a mixture of greens for various trees. We might add sunshine to the scene and lighten up an area of the fields that is highlighted by the sun. Then, we might add some blue sky and a few white clouds. So while we've used our imagination to create our image, we've also used an element of logic to tell us where to place the trees and fields and to select the most appropriate colours for the image.

An alternative way of combining logic and

imagination is to conjure up images that '**break the rules**' of logic. In this way we can create images that are **original,** and maybe **surreal.** For example, if we use our imagination again and conjure up the scene of fields and trees, we can choose to break the rules of logic by changing the colour of our images, so the fields become a vibrant pink and the trees become blue. We could also choose to change the shape of the trees and define their canopies as square rather than round. It's interesting to see the way we can interplay with logic and imagination, and it can additionally exercise both areas of our minds.

The above illustration may be recognisable as it relates to the concept of the 'artist's canvas' (discussed in the details of the Inspiration Accessory) where we can consciously build up the layers of an image and adapt those layers by viewing them as individual overlays. The above illustration, however, additionally highlights the way we can use our logic to interact with our imagination, and the way we can choose to **agree with or defy our logic** when we pursue creativity.

Memorising

Many books have been written to describe how we can improve our memories, so I won't go in to detail here. Instead, you will find two examples below for 'memorising with imagination', and once you've learned the principles, you can apply them to memorising many different types of information.

One method of memorising by using our imagination is to create **strange or funny pictures** in our minds of the information we're trying to remember. We can then piece our pictures together and create our own **storyline of information.** By creating a storyline, we're more likely to commit the information to memory, because we can remember pictures more easily than words alone, and we can create our own links from one picture to the next. An example of applying this method could be the creation of a storyline to remember the order of the eight planets from the sun:

> I visualise the **Sun** and imagine I'm holding it as a miniaturised version in my hands. A **Mercury** thermometer is sticking out of the mini-sun and shows it to be extremely hot. I place my mini-sun in the hands of a statue of **Venus**. The base of the statue is standing in a container filled with **Earth**. I notice a **Mars** bar wrapper lying on the floor near the statue. I see large feet by the wrapper and I look up and see **Jupiter**, the king of the gods. He's wearing a T-shirt which has S, U and N written on it, **Saturn, Uranus** and **Neptune**.

Now, see how quickly you can say, or write down, the order of the eight planets from the sun.

Another method for memorising with imagination is to remember **a code of images** that represent specific pieces of information, and then to apply that code to different situations. One type of code is to link images that have a similarity to the 'base' information we're trying to memorise. The image of an egg, for example, can be used as a code image for zero. An image of a walking stick can be used to represent the number 1, and so on:

0 = Egg
1 = Walking stick
2 = Swan
3 = Coat hook
4 = Chair
5 = Ice cream scoop
6 = Lawn mower
7 = Table
8 = Figure 8 on ice
9 = Balloon on a string

If we memorise the images for each of the numbers from nought to nine, then we have the ability to create a range of **storylines** for different number combinations. Have a look at the example below and see if you can work out the number combination:

> A man is cutting some grass with a lawnmower. He stops and walks over to a chair and sits down. He looks over at his garden pond and sees a swan moving on the water. He gets up

and walks into his house, collects his cap from the coat hook, and picks up his walking stick. Setting off down the road, he sees some children; one of them is holding a balloon on a string, and another is rolling an egg down the road.

The above story provides us with a method for remembering a specific number combination. Memorising coded images for numbers can be even more useful where number combinations are long or obscure. Of course, these coded images can have their foul ups, such as if we forget the storyline or we can't remember the code for the images. However, it's still a very useful tool. By the way, the number combination for the above story is 6 4 2 3 1 9 0 (lawnmower, chair, swan, coat hook, walking stick, balloon on a string, and egg).

We can use our imagination to memorise a huge diversity of information just by using the principle of assigning images and using a storyline. Of course, we can't use this method for everything we want to memorise, but we can at least be aware of it, and then choose to apply it when we decide.

Motivating

Another way we can use our imagination is to motivate ourselves. An example might be someone who is motivated to work overtime, so they can earn extra money and buy the car of their dreams. If they visualise their dream car and use this to motivate themselves, then they are likely to buy their car sooner, because they're aiming towards their envisioned goal. Of course, the success of using our imagination as a motivational tool depends on how passionate and determined we are about achieving our particular goals. We need to have the commitment to follow through with our goals, and keep them prominent in our minds, if we want to move them forwards. Equally, if we regularly use our imagination as a motivational tool, then we can **strengthen our resolve** to achieve our envisioned goals. This is why our imagination can become a **great source of personal strength,** because despite what anyone else says, *we* can be the person in charge of our envisioned goals, and *we* can be the person who is motivated and determined to achieve them.

Another example of using imagination for motivation is the way some professional swimmers visualise themselves before and during a competition. Firstly, they visualise very carefully an authentic image of a swimming pool, and then they visualise the swimmers that will be competing in the race. Taking their time, they visualise actually swimming in the race together with the other swimmers, and feel themselves physically swimming and implementing their strategies. As the race continues and the final laps approach, they feel an extra surge of energy, until finally, they see themselves winning the race. Some

Imagination Accessory

professional swimmers even imagine they're being chased by a shark so that they can raise their adrenalin levels and motivate themselves even further. Of course, this type of visualisation has to be done much more slowly and precisely than the way I've described. The visualiser has to really 'feel' themselves there, both physically and mentally, and they need to take sufficient time to make the visualisation as real as possible.

A different version of using imagination for motivation is visualising where we want to be in a few years' time. We might visualise where we want to be in our career, or where we want our passions to take us, or the type of lifestyle we'd like to be living. The idea behind this is that if we visualise where we want to be, then we can establish our goals more precisely, and then we can set them within a defined timeline.

Another point to note is that when we motivate our minds through our imagination, we're also anticipating what we will feel when we achieve our goals. For example, we might feel that a new car will give us a sense of freedom and independence, particularly if it's the first car we've ever had. As a professional swimmer, we might feel that winning a particular race will make us feel proud of ourselves, and for our country. We might feel that changing our lifestyle will help us to be healthier and happier. The **anticipated feelings** of the goals we envisage can strengthen our resolve to achieve them.

Rehearsing

Closely linked to 'motivating our minds with imagination' is the way we can use our imagination to **rehearse** a scene. We might be rehearsing how to ask for a pay rise, or giving our reasons for writing a particular article. In both situations we have the capacity to visualise our scenes, together with what we might say and the reaction of the other people. The ability to rehearse a scene in our minds is an extremely valuable skill, because we can attempt to **anticipate the obstacles** we might encounter and we can try to generate some **positive outcomes**. A useful example is to consider the scenario of public speaking. Much of the fear of public speaking is related to anticipated fears, such as forgetting what we're going to say, or stumbling over our words, or feeling extremely nervous. But if we use our imagination to rehearse a presentation, then we can begin to break down our negative thoughts and turn them into positive thoughts and positive outcomes.

If we stay with the public speaking scenario for a moment, we can say that a very important point for visualising such a scenario is to **think BIG**. We need to make sure when we visualise ourselves public speaking that everything is on a grand scale. So we visualise we're in a large conference centre, with a large number of people, and a large stage on which to make our speech. The idea is that we need to *maximise* what makes us most nervous about public speaking and confront it 'head on' in our visualisations. If we visualise ourselves in a situation that might initially seem very scary, then having coped with our visualisation, we should then be able to cope more easily when we face it in reality. Another important point is to bring in as many emotions and senses as we can with the images we visualise. The reason for this is to make our visualisations feel as real as possible.

To give you an idea of rehearsing with imagination, a conference presentation scenario is provided below. As you read through the descriptions, slowly visualise each of the details described, and really see the images in your mind. Also, try to feel some of the emotions and senses that are included in the descriptions, and add some of your own as you become more aware of them. Try to see and feel yourself actually giving the presentation and absorbing the passion and energy of your audience.

The Conference Presentation

You're standing in the conference room where you'll soon be giving your presentation. At the moment, the room is empty, so you take the opportunity to absorb your surroundings.

From the platform at the front of the room, you look at the seats where your audience will be sitting. The seats are blue, and are gradually tiered upwards towards the back of the room so that every person can have a clear view of the speaker. There are four aisles between the rows of seats, and you notice the red carpeting that highlights their locations. You're aware of the sheer size of the place; the high ceilings, banks of lights, and huge presentation screen. You become very familiar with the layout of the room and decide to walk along one of the aisles. As you walk slowly up the aisle, you turn to your right and sit down on one of the blue seats. You notice how comfortable they feel, far better than the plastic seats at some of the other venues you've attended. From here you can see the platform quite clearly, and you imagine seeing yourself making your speech. After absorbing your present surroundings, you stand up and walk slowly back to the speaker's platform. At this moment, you have a few butterflies in your stomach, but you don't feel too nervous.

Some time later

You notice it's now only half an hour before you give your presentation. You sit quietly in one of the front row seats and begin to hear people entering the room. At first, you hear a general background hum of people settling into their seats, shuffling papers, and having the occasional chat. People who've suddenly recognised each other move quickly from one seat to another and catch up with the latest news. As you sit in your comfortable chair, you feel a few flashes of excitement, and your adrenaline levels start to rise as you think about the key points of your presentation. You look briefly around the room and see that it's packed to capacity; about 400 people. Although you feel a little nervous, you feel passionate about what you're going to say, and you're keen to grab the attention of your audience.

Getting ready to present

As everyone begins to settle down, a general hush is heard around the room; only a few coughs remain to break the quietened surrounds. The host of the conference presentation introduces you to the audience, and you breathe deeply to settle your last minute nerves. As the introduction concludes, you stand to the applause of the audience, and approach the podium. As you begin to start talking with confidence and clarity, you know you've immediately attracted the attention of the audience. You start to really enjoy talking about something you know really well, and which you're passionate about. You look over at the audience and engage them regularly as you speak.

Towards the end of your presentation

While you keep within the allotted time given, you feel you could go on talking about your topic because you feel so passionate and confident. At the end of your presentation, you receive a resounding applause and you acknowledge your achievement. You feel a sense of accomplishment, and you look forward to the next opportunity when you can speak in public and convey the value of your words.

Speaking in public, and doing it well, is one of the biggest achievements that many people can make in their lives. When we realise that we all have a **significant contribution to make in life**, then we can begin to release the knowledge and the words that are within us, and learn to convey them for the benefit of others.

Sport

I've already mentioned the way professional swimmers use their imagination to motivate themselves. There are also many other ways in which imagination is used in sport, and sports researchers have undertaken numerous projects to assess the ways in which imagination can be of benefit. For example, in one project, some sports researchers wanted to assess if there were any benefits of soccer players visualising themselves dribbling a ball between a number of cones. In order to do this realistically in their minds, the soccer players were first required to physically dribble the ball, and second required to sit down, close their eyes, and visualise their actions. In both the physical and the visualised situations, they had to move the ball as quickly and as accurately as possible, and they were required to incorporate their senses and emotions to make the visualisations seem as real as possible. When the sports researchers assessed both the physical and the visualised situations, their results revealed that in the visualised situation, the brain of each player produced the same mental effect as if they were physically moving the ball.

Learning to visualise in this way is an important skill for people in sport because it can enable them to deal far better with their nerves, particularly when it comes to pressurised situations. Research has shown that when an athlete becomes nervous, they can potentially tense up to a point where they often fail, partly because their minds tell them they *can* fail. When an athlete tenses up, their brain recognises that tension, and their actions can become stilted, as if they were learning their skills for the first time. Looking at the brain when this actually happens shows that the brain is operating from the section where we first learn a skill, so the actions of a nervous player are more likely to be stilted. On the other hand, if athletes use their visualisation skills and confidently see themselves succeeding, then they are better equipped to control their minds and much more likely to do well.

The moral of the above example is that for each of our goals we need to **visualise and rehearse our success** long before we get there. If we use our imagination and rehearse the success of our goals, then we have a greater opportunity to work confidently towards them and we can restrict the negative thoughts that can so often take us away from where we want to be.

Relaxing

Another way we can use our imagination is to help us to relax. For example, have a look at the scene below and think about how you might feel if you were really in that place:

> You're on holiday on a warm tropical island. You're relaxing on a cosy sun lounger, gently sipping an ice cool drink. You feel the warmth of the air touching your face, and a large umbrella shades you from the midday sun. As you pick up your novel and continue to read, your sense of smell is alerted by the wonderful aromas emanating from the outdoor barbecues. The hotel chefs are preparing a lunch time feast, with various meats, prawns, peppers, tomatoes, and salads….it's simply sheer relaxation.

By using our imagination, we can conjure up many different relaxing scenes and use these as a way of calming down our lives. We can make our images very real in our minds, and by doing so, we can help ourselves **to relax as we concentrate on our images** rather than focus on our worries of the day. Relaxing our minds doesn't mean falling asleep or trying not to think about anything at all, it's about **taking our minds on a holiday** and visualising images that help us unwind.

Here's another scene you could create in your mind:

> I'm sitting in an apple orchard on a gentle summer's day. Relaxing in my deck chair, I enjoy the warmth of the late afternoon sun. I feel the very slightest of breezes cooling and touching my face. I look up at one of the apple trees, and I watch the apples ripen from green to red; the speed of time passes in a different way in this place... sometimes slow... sometimes fast. I sense myself taking a bite from one of the juicy red apples; I can taste its sweetness, and some of the juice runs down my chin.

When you want to unwind and relax, you can visit one of the places you've created in your mind or think of somewhere entirely new. You can study the details of your images, senses, and emotions, and move away from the details of your worries. And you can give your mind permission to concentrate on your places for relaxation. When you eventually come back to reality, you should feel more refreshed and energised.

Create a place for mental relaxation:
Have a go at creating a place in your mind which you can visit for relaxation. Record the details of the place so that you can remember them clearly. And as with the previous types of visualisation, bring your emotions and senses with you so you can make your scenes as real as possible.

SELECTIONS AND VIEWS

Selecting a Surface

We've already learned about the artist's canvas as a way of seeing in our minds. Through the artist's canvas we can build up layers of a picture, and then we can change our picture by taking away certain layers and replacing them with new layers. Understanding the method of the artist's canvas can give us the opportunity to see how we might construct certain images in our minds.

Another aspect of constructing our images is to think about the surface we select. When we imagine a detailed description, we often select a surface in our minds so that we can transpose our images onto that surface and gradually build up our layers. For example, if we use our imagination to decorate a bedroom (*and take our time to really visualise what we see*) then we can place our selected images over the surface of that room and gradually watch it take shape:

> Imagine a room with white walls, a ceiling, and a floor. Paint two opposing walls purple, and the other two walls beige. Paint the ceiling white, and attach an opaque oval light fitting in the centre of the ceiling. Install fitted pine wardrobes within one of the purple painted walls. On the opposite side of the fitted wardrobes, place a double bed with a headboard of pine. Lay down a carpet of a delicate violet colour, and notice the way it blends with the purple walls. Put a bed side table to the left of the bed, and place a vase of yellow flowers on top of the table, and three books piled on top of each other.

While reading through the above description, you created a surface of four walls, a ceiling, and a floor, and then placed the colours and furniture within that surface. You may have assumed that the walls were straight, rather than curved, and that the four walls enclosed the room entirely, because you drew this from your memory of what a room should look like. If you took your time to visualise the room, you would have seen it quite clearly, and even added your own details to the descriptions to make the images stronger in your mind. For instance, what type of vase did you visualise and what type of flowers did you have? The description only said there was a vase of yellow flowers, it didn't describe the shape or detail of the vase and it didn't name the type of flowers in the vase. Nevertheless, you created these additional details in your mind, and that was partly because the details helped you to better visualise the scene. By the way, did you make any space for a door? (Some people do and some people don't).

If I asked you to imagine another room with red painted walls, a fireplace, and a candelabra, you'll probably be more aware of placing these images on a surface in your mind. You may also be more aware of some of the assumptions you make about the information which is given, such as the shape and size of the room described, where the candelabra should hang, and the location of the fireplace. Selecting our surface and giving ourselves certain **assumptions** enables us to quickly form an image in our minds and to add other details in the very instant they are described.

We know we can select our images of the candelabra and the fireplace from our Visual Encyclopaedia. When we select those images, we have a vague notion of what our fireplace and candelabra might look like, but without further description from the narrator, **we add our own details to the images** so that we can see them more clearly in our minds. By adding this additional detail, we actually create the opportunity of studying our images more closely, such as being able to **zoom in** on the candelabra and to notice the individual droplets that make up the candelabra, maybe even the different colours of light as they reflect from the sparkling glass. It's fascinating to learn about the sheer capacity of the details we store in our Visual Encyclopaedia, and the range of choices we can make with our images. In fact, it's only through *this* level of appreciation that we can understand how one person's image of the red room might show a green marble fireplace and an opulent chandelier, while another person's image might show a dark timber fireplace and a very small, delicate chandelier. Because we're only given a few details about the furniture in the room, the images of the fireplace and the chandelier are likely to be different for each of us. So when we select a surface in our minds, the image we ultimately see will depend on the assumptions we make about that surface, as well as the individual details we apply.

Another interesting exercise relating to the surfaces we create is to think about the way we visualise a face. If it's someone we know, then our minds use our knowledge of what a face should look like, and then keeps searching for the image we're looking for. We're aware of placing the eyes, nose, and mouth on the surface of our face, and while we might not be able to bring our picture into clear focus, we can attempt to get **the essence of our image**. If a narrator actually gives us the description of a face, then we can use our knowledge of that surface to create the features described. It might be a man with a pale face, pointed nose, big brown eyes, and a slim straight mouth. With only these few words we can begin to define the features of our face, and we can enhance these features as additional details are given by the narrator and/or by ourselves. We might not be able to 'hold' our picture perfectly in our minds, but we can keep the essence of the features we're aware of.

It's worth mentioning that we can test some of the assumptions we make about selected mental images if we attempt to physically draw what we see in our minds. For example, have you ever tried to draw someone's face and found that you've placed the eyes way too high? That's because we *think* we know where the eyes sit, but in reality, it's quite different. When people first learn to draw and paint, one of the most important lessons they can learn is to really 'look' at their subject and to draw what they 'see', rather than what their minds assume.

A final note on selecting surfaces in our minds is to consider the exploration of possibilities **outside of our normal assumptions**. In this way we can take our imagination beyond the descriptions which are given, and create new and original images, some of which may take us in new directions. For example, we could consider the red room again and instead of making it a square room, we could make it an oval room. We could then place the candelabra at one end of the room instead of in the centre. And we could allow a book to float freely around the room. This might sound a bit strange, but the principle is about understanding the assumptions we make about our descriptions so that we can choose to turn them around and create our own possibilities and outcomes. We can apply this principle when we want to be creative, particularly if we want to be original in our work.

Viewing angles in our minds

The other point to make about the images we construct in our imagination is that we have the option to choose a variety of viewing angles, although some of these will depend on the type of images we're attempting to see. If we consider again the first room we visualised as described above (the decorated bedroom), we will have changed our viewing angle several times as we built up our image. Before the bed enters the room, we are just in a space, concentrating on the colours of the walls. Then as the details of the painted walls and furniture emerge, we are able to 'fix' on various points for viewing the furniture and the room. By the time the room is finished, we can view it from different angles and zoom in on specific details.

We all have a favourite viewing angle, and we tend to keep this angle as we build up our image. Our viewing angle is an interesting aspect of our imagination because it has implications for the outcome of what we see. For example, if you viewed the room from the back of the bed, then the bedside table would be on your left if you were lying on the bed, but if you viewed the room looking towards the bed, then the table would be on the right if you were lying on the bed. So when we use our imagination, we often use our own interpretations, apply additional details, and select our own viewing angles. This enables us to visualise the images in our minds much more clearly.

If we now move on to the second room we visualised above (the red room), we can again consider our viewing angles. We can choose to look down from the ceiling, or look up at the ceiling, or look at one of the red painted walls. At first this might be a little difficult for us to visualise, but if we add detail to our images then it becomes much easier for us to focus on our different viewing angles. It's through the **detail** that we can '**fix and focus**' on our images.

When you changed the shape of the red room to oval, how did you see it? Because it's a shape we aren't used to for a bedroom, it can be a little difficult for us to view and to keep in our minds. When I visualised it, I saw the oval by looking over the top of the room, as if it had no ceiling, and strangely, there was nothing else on the outside of that room, mostly because I didn't ask my mind to visualise anything else.

We can do all sorts of tricks with our viewing angles. We can take our square or oval red room and rotate it around in our minds, rather like the **360**

degree images on a computer. If we add more furniture to our room, such as a sofa, coffee table, vase of flowers, and a selection of books, then we can view our image from even more angles because we can 'fix and focus' on the details. We could look towards the sofa and see the coffee table in front of the sofa, and a vase of red roses sitting in the centre of the coffee table. Alternatively, we could look the other way and see a dark timber fireplace and the red painted wall. Artists, photographers, and film makers often use the ability of 'viewing angles' in their imagination when they want to search for images that are original, fresh, or even quirky. For example, instead of taking a photograph of a group of flowers with a conventional 'side on' angle, a photographer might decide to use a different angle and take a photograph from beneath a group of flowers, looking upwards towards the sky. The possibilities of viewing angles in our minds are numerous because we aren't constrained by the limitations of our reality.

ADAPTING THE WAY WE THINK

At last it feels like we're really uncovering some useful abilities of our imagination and learning how to apply our Accessory in a wider capacity. We've learned that one of the key ways we can see our imagination is by adapting the images we see from reality. We've also learned about some of the ways we can use our imagination, such as to motivate, rehearse, and relax.

Another important ability is the way we can use our imagination to plan things in our minds, such as thinking about the jobs we have to do or the places we have to be. But as well as all of these amazing abilities, we need to add one more very important aspect to our discussion, and that is, the way we can use our imagination to *think*.

Our imagination gives us a unique opportunity to open our minds, not only to images,sensations, and emotions, but also to new thoughts and ideas. Using our imagination as a way of thinking means that we can allow our minds to **think in an unrestrained way**. We can move away from the conventional pattern of our thoughts and open our minds to a free flow of thoughts. So while we often use logic to come up with options for a particular issue, if we also use our imagination, then we can **widen the scope of our options** and include possibilities that might at first glance seem impossible.

One of the most well known phrases that encourages the use of **imaginative thinking** is the phrase '**think outside the square**' (sometimes termed as 'think outside the box'). It's a phrase that's often coined as a way of telling people to think beyond their conventional patterns of thought. So instead of thinking purely within the square, where our conventional thoughts exist, we are encouraged to take our minds outside the square and into a new world of thoughts and paths. On the surface, it might sound quite an easy thing to do, but because our minds are designed to recognise and organise information into patterns, trying to think in an unconventional way can actually feel quite difficult. **Thinking in patterns** is very important for our minds because it means we can do things quickly without having to learn them from scratch, but if we don't ever learn to think beyond those patterns, then we can limit the scope of our possibilities, and we might even limit our own potential. We need to learn to **adapt the way we think** and look beyond our conventional patterns of thought and the patterns of our lives.

Another well known expression for thinking with our imagination is '**lateral thinking**', a term which gained prominence in the 1970's through the work of people such as Edward de Bono. Since that time, the application of lateral thinking has become much more widely acknowledged as a means of **looking beyond our normal considerations** in order to come up with new thoughts and different ways of seeing a particular issue.

So we have imaginative thinking and lateral thinking and the expression 'think outside the square', all of which mean the same thing: to think in an unrestrained way so that we can come up with new thoughts, new ideas, new directions, new methods, etc. It's important for us to understand and use our imaginative thinking because if we do this, we can learn how to apply it more easily and increase our potential for using it. Sometimes we can find ourselves going round and round in circles as we try to solve a problem, but it's often because we're using the same thinking patterns that we've always used. We can allow ourselves to go further and further down a particular path not realising that there might be an easier or more effective solution. So if we learn to use our imaginative thinking more often, then we can allow our minds to come up with **different perspectives** and increase our opportunities for **breaking new ground**.

Applying Imaginative Thinking

Our pure imagination is unrestrained, we don't say to it *"this can't be done"* or *"what a stupid idea";* we allow our imagination to freely flow with images, thoughts, and ideas. This lack of restraint in our imagination is the reason why it's such a unique and valuable method of thinking. If we restrain our imagination then we restrain our potential for seeing new ways of dealing with a particular issue. Even Aristotle, a Greek philosopher and scientist (384-322 BC), said that *"plausible impossibilities should be preferred to unconvincing possibilities."* He was saying that we should use our imagination to consider different ways of approaching a problem or issue. He was telling us to think outside of our normal considerations, and to consider those possibilities that might at first glance seem impossible. We wouldn't have discovered many of the other countries in the world if all mankind had considered the world to be flat, with no other possibility.

When we apply our imaginative thinking, we first allow ourselves to come up with *all* of our **options,** and only then do we analyse them and weigh them up. Creating options when we're trying to solve a particular problem, or attempting to create something new, is essential if we want to take our thinking patterns in different directions. *But how do we come up with those options?* Well, one of the most useful ways is to **brainstorm our ideas**, something which is common practice in many businesses and teaching establishments today. When we brainstorm, we allow our minds to pick anything and everything about a particular topic so that we can keep that free flow of thoughts going. We might be brainstorming on our own or in a group, and this partly depends on the subject matter and what we're trying to discover. But the main principle is that we keep on brainstorming for as long as we have ideas to offer.

An example of a brainstorming session might be collecting a group of shoppers together and asking them how a specific supermarket could be improved. With the subject matter in mind, the shoppers might come up with the following ideas:

Improve the labelling of products to state whether they contain ingredients such as peanuts, gluten, or egg, to assist those with food allergies.

Provide display areas of products that cater for other dietary needs, such as low sugar content, low sodium content, dairy free, or soya products. This would assist the shopper in recognising certain brands.

Increase the variety of 'single portion' foods to cater for the market of single people. Ensure these portions are easily identifiable within the supermarket.

Create a section of the supermarket for 'meal of the week' and contain all the ingredients that would be needed to make that meal for a family of four.

Improve signage from the ceiling to indicate a wider range of products.

Improve the visibility of signage by using large white letters on a green background.

Increase the variety of 'low fat' foods and identify them clearly in the supermarket.

If we say that the above list of suggestions is absolutely everything the shoppers can think of, and the brainstorming of ideas is completely exhausted, we can then introduce another way of searching their minds for ideas. If we now asked the shoppers to

brainstorm with specific images of shopping at the supermarket, then we can **heighten their level of conscious awareness** and attempt to gain additional feedback. For example, we could ask them to imagine themselves arriving at the supermarket and then ask them to identify any problems or improvements that could be made. We could ask them to imagine themselves using a shopping trolley and making their way around the supermarket. We ask them *"What do you see?" "What problems do you encounter?" "What's on your shopping list?" "Can you find everything you're looking for?"* By giving the shoppers an imaginary situation, they have the opportunity to recreate the supermarket scenario and to recall issues and problems they may have encountered at some time. Having undertaken this imaginary exercise, the shoppers might come up with the following additional comments:

> The aisles are too narrow for two trolleys to pass comfortably.

> They're always running out of products on the shelves and not refilling them quickly enough.

> They never have my brand of processed peas, so I have to go to another supermarket to get them.

> I've never been able to find any shoe polish.

When we brainstorm with specific images and heighten our level of conscious awareness, we can **place ourselves within the subject being discussed** and allow ourselves the opportunity to create new thoughts. It's very natural for us to see images in our minds when we think about a subject which is the focus of a brainstorming session, but unless we place an emphasis on **consciously visualising** our images, then we may be limiting our thoughts. It's always an interesting exercise in a brainstorming session to ask people to think of as many ideas as they can, and then when all the ideas are exhausted, to introduce specific images that can heighten their level of conscious awareness. Invariably, they will have more ideas to add to the subject.

This process of consciously visualising specific images is a principle that we can apply in many different situations. Having images in our minds helps us to *think* about our subject, and the more conscious we are of those images, the more we can use them.

Options

Once we have all of our ideas from a brainstorming session, we can then formulate them into clear sentences and give ourselves the opportunity to consider our options. A much used method for doing this is to **weigh up the pros and cons** of tackling an option, and to 'rule in' or 'rule out' each option before we spend any lengthy time or money on them.

This doesn't mean that we rule out an option because it's considered to be impossible, we only rule them out based on the **criteria we've selected**, such as financial limits, time limits, quality controls, personnel requirements, level of expertise, etc.

Too often, businesses can find themselves steam rolling ahead with what they *think* is the best option for a particular issue, only to learn from experience that it hasn't proved to be successful. They can spend an enormous amount of time trying to make their chosen option successful, when in fact they might be working with the *wrong* option. If we use our Imaginative Thinking via brainstorming and via images that heighten our level of conscious awareness, then we can bring in other methods of thinking, such as logic and analysis, and work towards choosing options that will prove more successful in their outcomes. So we have to inform ourselves about *all* of our options before we can attempt to formulate and 'run' with them.

OPENING OUR MINDS

This section contains four exercises, each of which are designed to open your mind in a specific way. They draw on much of the knowledge you've gained so far about your Imagination Accessory, and they aim to improve your imagination even further.

Observing and Thinking

Exercise 1 – Observe, Record, Adapt

The basis of Exercise 1 'Observe, Record, Adapt' is to use your **conscious observation** to record the details of selected images, and later to call up those images so that you can adapt them with your imagination. You might select your images at home, on your way to work, during a lunch break, or maybe on a leisurely walk. It's best to collect between one and three images, but no more than this, otherwise you'll overload your mind and defeat the object of the exercise. To get a better idea of how to use this exercise, the following is an example:

> You're going to take your dog for a walk, and you decide to consciously Observe and Record some of the images you see along the way. As you take your usual and familiar route towards your local park, you notice more consciously a large tree on the corner of the road. It has a huge canopy and a dark trunk that has become twisted over time. You decide that this is one of the pictures you will Observe and Record in your visual memory, and you consciously record the details. This is your first mental picture.
>
> A little while later, you find yourself walking around the park and notice some leaves on the ground. You decide to study a few of them and record their shapes, varying colours, and twisted edges. This is your second mental picture.

As you're walking with your dog on the way home, you notice a bright red door on the front of a white washed house. The contrast is so striking that you decide to record the details in your mind; the four distinctive panels of the door, the gold door knocker in the shape of a lion's head, and the white step below the front door. This is your third mental picture.

Later that evening, you decide to think again about your three mental pictures. You're able to visualise all three of them and record much of the detail you observed. You think about adapting each picture in turn. With the tree, you imagine children climbing the long outstretched branches. With the leaves, you imagine them flying in the wind, but in slow motion rather than normal speed, and you can still discern the details of their shapes and colours. With the red door, you imagine the head of the lion saying "hello" as it greets you at the door.

Whatever the images and however small or large they are, the idea is to Observe and Record what you see around you, and then to Adapt those images as you exercise your imagination. If you actively use Exercise 1, then you will automatically find that your imagination will begin to expand. You will begin to see things around you in a different way and observe much more of the life around you. Your ability to remember visual details should also improve, and you can begin to develop your ability to 'switch on' your imagination as and when you choose.

Exercise 2 – Sharpen your Visualisation Skills

Sometimes our ability to visualise might feel so inactive that we don't know how to get it started again. One way of stimulating our visualisation skills is to think of a few words that describe objects, such as a lemon, car, tree, fork, glove, book, and then to consciously see those objects in our minds. By carrying out this simple exercise we can sharpen our ability to visualise, and also exercise our mental screen.

Exercise 3 – Look for the Details

Another way to sharpen our visualisation skills is to look for the details in our images. For example, imagine the details in the following scene:

> A candle sits on a dark wood table. It's a slim white candle set in a silver stand. The silver stand is about two inches high and is designed to represent a mini Greek column, with fluting down the sides and a solid base. The candle is lit and has an orange flame. Occasionally, the flame of the candle flickers as the air moves around it. As the glow of the flame grows, you

notice the yellow and orange colours, and a feint blue colour at the base of the flame.

By concentrating on the details of the candle, we can sharpen the images in our minds and sharpen our visualisation skills.

Exercise 4 – Use Trigger Words

Another exercise for your imagination is to select five words at random and include all of those words in a short story. You could select your words from a dictionary or ask five people to give you one word each. The process is entirely up to you. Using these trigger words is a good way of coming up with something entirely original, and it's one of the very best ways of exercising your imagination.

Here are the five words I came up with: Concrete, Treasure, Chair, Ernie, Polka.

Exercise 5 – Add Senses and Emotions

The final exercise is about selecting words that conjure up senses and emotions, and then composing a short paragraph that represents each of those words. For example, by using the word 'blustery' you might come up with something like this:

> As I walk along the pavement on a cold blustery winter's day, I try to keep warm, and pull my

coat tightly around me. I pull my woollen hat over my head and try to cover my ears to defend them against the cold. As I continue to battle through the wind, I notice some leaves rushing past me and others whirling around my feet………

Now think of the word 'magical'. How would you represent that word? What images would you choose? What colours would you see? What emotions and senses would you feel?

Some other examples to choose from include: Dreamy, Dynamic, Placid, Clear, Hazy, Strong, Calm, Adventurous.

Senses more Specifically

You could also imagine more specifically your senses of taste, touch, smell, and sound and try to heighten them in your imagination. You could choose one example and explore all of your senses in relation to this one example, such as biting into some fresh pineapple… Will it be sweet? Will it be sour? Imagine the texture of the pineapple… Is it tough? Is it soft and smooth? What about the smell of the pineapple? Is there another type of fruit that has a similar smell? And then imagine the sound of biting into the pineapple and listening as you chew… Is it crunchy, or soft and pliable? What does it sound like?

Emotions more specifically

You could practice calling up emotions in your imagination, such as feeling calm, content, vibrant, or energetic, and then give yourself some time to concentrate on each of these feelings. Allow a gradual change for imagining each emotion, and in particular give yourself some time when you change from a very calm emotion to a very energetic emotion, and vice versa. Try to focus on each of your chosen emotions and spend time with them in your imagination. Try to really 'feel' them and understand them in your mind.

CONCLUSION

When we think about our imagination, how it works and how we use it in our everyday lives, we can begin to appreciate how **complex** and **unique** it really is. We've learned about the way we can see with our imagination and how we can convert descriptive details into our own **visual, sensual, and emotional dialogue**. We've also seen how imagination can transport our minds forwards in time, backwards in time, or keep us somewhere in the present. And we've learned that we can think **freely and unrestrained** with our imagination and create images, ideas, and options that we might never have considered if we had restrained our thought processes with logic, or by the limitations of what we already know. These qualities are just some of the highlights of an Accessory that is sometimes beyond our comprehension, but one which we can endeavour to explore and uncover, and use more widely in our lives.

Key Points

Our imagination doesn't exist in a vacuum; much of what we see in our imagination comes first from our visual memory.

Our visual memory helps us to 'record and recall' our images.

We can plan things in our minds through the use of our visual memory e.g. when we think about preparing a meal.

Our Visual Encyclopaedia enables us to 'label' our images and to add senses and emotions.

We retain a memory of touch, taste, smell, and sound, and we can recall these in our minds.

We retain a memory of emotions, and we can stimulate a particular emotion by recalling a personal experience.

Key Points

We have the potential to record new sounds in our imagination.

Many of the images we see in our imagination are adapted from our images of reality.

Enhancing the images in our imagination with detail, senses, and emotions can make them stronger and clearer in our minds.

If we try to visualise an image which isn't in our visual memory, then we might not be seeing the 'correct' image.

Authentic Visualisation allows us to visualise our reality.

Some of the uses of Authentic Visualisation include recalling the places we know, visualising the jobs we need to do, recalling a personal memory, and unwinding from our day.

Adapted Visualisation allows us to change the images we've recorded from reality.

Some of the uses of Adapted Visualisation include visualising our goals, motivating our minds, being creative, memorising information, and rehearsing a scene.

Key Points

Our mind's eye allows us to see images on our own mental screen.

We can actively project images onto our mental screen and view them like a movie.

We can choose to view our images like an artist's canvas and build up layers of different images.

We can choose to control the speed of the images we place on our mental screen and we can add more detail to make them clearer.

Our sensual and emotional memories can be thought of as Memory Cards on which we record the details of our experiences.

The ability to imagine senses and emotions will depend in part on how much we 'focus' on memorising and recalling them.

We can imagine TTSS senses authentically and adaptively.

We define our emotions very broadly; imagining a specific emotion can help us to find some of the layers that rest inside that emotion.

Imagining and meditating with a certain emotion can actually convince us that we feel a certain way.

Key Points

> We can imagine our emotions authentically and adaptively.

Conscious imagination enables us to have more control over our images, senses, emotions, and thoughts, and this is particularly useful for creativity.

Subconscious imagination enables us to come up with images, sounds, and thoughts that we might never have thought of at a conscious level.

In our sleeping dreams, our imagination can encompass images, senses, and emotions, and we can even create our own dialogue.

We have the potential to connect with our sleeping dreams in three different ways: as the viewer; appearing as ourselves; and appearing as someone or something else.

In our sleepy dream states, we can sometimes take control of our imagination and influence our outcomes.

We can generate our imagination from many different sources, including novels, music, and paintings.

We can bring our life experiences into our imagination when we read a novel.

Key Points

We can complement our imagination with selected inspirational sources to assist us in creativity.

Our imagination can help us to plan our creative ideas, practice with different options, and learn from our thoughts.

We can use logic and imagination to create something 'appropriate', but we can also create something 'inappropriate' by breaking the rules of logic.

We can memorise with our imagination by visualising strange or funny images of the information we're trying to remember, and then piece them together to create a storyline.

Motivating our minds through our imagination can help us to strengthen our resolve to achieve our goals.

Rehearsing a scene in our imagination can help us to anticipate potential obstacles; we can then attempt to create positive outcomes.

For each of our goals, we need to visualise and rehearse our success long before we achieve it.

We can relax with our imagination by visiting places we create in our minds.

Key Points

When we select a surface in our imagination we can place specific details on that surface.

Giving ourselves certain assumptions about our images helps us to form them more quickly.

We add our own details to the descriptions that are given so that we can see them more clearly in our minds.

We can zoom in on the details of the images we create.

In knowing the assumptions we can make about our images, we can explore the possibilities outside of our normal assumptions and create new and original images and thoughts.

The details of our images help us to 'fix and focus' on what we see, and they can also help us to explore different viewing angles.

> Using our imagination as a way of thinking means that we can think in an unrestrained way and widen the scope of our options.

> To be creative and to open our minds, we need to adapt the way we think and to look beyond our conventional patterns of thought.

Key Points

If we brainstorm with specific images, we can heighten our level of conscious awareness and place ourselves within the subject being discussed.

We need to consider *all* of our options and weigh them up before we choose our paths.

Meet the Author

Overview

Angela is a published Author, Speaker and Urban Designer. Passionate about helping people uncover their Mind Potential, she takes you on a journey as you begin to realise your amazing possibilities. "When we're given appropriate tools to access areas of our minds, then we have the potential to discover **new skills**, to broaden our **individuality** and to strengthen our **commonality**."

She describes how we can grow the potential of our minds, so that we can unravel our many talents and learn to use our minds more effectively. Through the use of what she calls 'Mind Accessories', Angela shows how we can learn to access our minds in a way that can expand our capacity for Learning, Creating, Inspiring, Imagining, and much more.

How did the Mind Books begin?

Angela's interest in the mind started when she began to realise we need additional ways of thinking and learning, and we need to improve our understanding of working 'with' our minds, rather than against them. Her career in Town Planning and Urban Design assisted in this process, as in addition to logic and application, she learned to expand her spatial, analytical, and lateral thinking skills, and learned to visualise different dimensions of the urban environment. She also researched numerous books and articles on the mind, and reviewed and critiqued various concepts on Thinking, Learning and Application.

"I've always been fascinated by the mind, particularly how we can access and improve our mental abilities, and how we can move beyond the boundaries we often place on ourselves. Many of us are unaware of the enormous capabilities of our minds."

Through her continued research and analysis, Angela began to grow ideas for the way information can be Understood, Accessed and Applied. She created a series of exercises and techniques and tested these with a range of individuals. As a result, many of these individuals were able to expand the world they thought they knew, and to activate other areas in their lives. This enabled Angela to refine ways of understanding and uncovering various processes for Learning, Creating, Inspiring, Imagining, and other important qualities.

The culmination of Angela's investigations led to her concept of 'Mind Accessories', a process through which different aspects of our lives can be considered and activated in our minds, allowing thoughts and ideas to flourish, mental activities to broaden, and actions to be defined.

Her Mind Books are available in paperback or as eBooks at Amazon in Australia, UK and US, and at other eStores. A **Fiction Novel** is also on the way, an area of writing she had never considered until she had Viewed her World Differently through **Accessorise your Mind**.

* * *

You can find Angela at her website
and at various social media sites.

https://angelaclareauthor.wordpress.com/

Endnotes

[1] Penguin Classics (1996) Jane Eyre by Charlotte Bronte, Penguin Books Ltd, London: pages 100 to 101. 'Jane Eyre' was first published in 1847.

[2] 'The Arnolfini Marriage' was painted by Jan van Eyck (c.1390-1441) somewhere between 1432 and 1439. The painting provides us with vivid colours, accurately rendered textures, and an illusion of three dimensional space on a two dimensional canvas. A mystery remains in the painting as to the identity of the two people shown in the mirror which is located in the background of the scene.

[3] 'I Paint a Picture of You' describes the way we can bring images, thoughts, and emotions into our minds and form a 'picture' of someone who is well known and who we admire. The picture we paint in our minds can be influenced by the media, but if that person inspires us, then we have the opportunity to adjust our 'picture' and factor in the qualities we perceive in that person – we can move away from the media banner.

[4] 'The Alfresco Painting' is the result of sitting in many an alfresco setting and having enjoyed the ambience of such places. It's intriguing to consider what an alfresco painting might depict and how it might capture the feelings and thoughts of such places.

[5] Penguin Classics (1996) Jane Eyre by Charlotte Bronte, Penguin Books Ltd, London: pages 28 to 29.

[6] Claude Debussy (1862-1918) took two years to write 'La mer'. He completed it in 1905.

www.ingramcontent.com/pod-product-compliance
Lightning Source LLC
Chambersburg PA
CBHW070533090426
42735CB00013B/2966